KANJIZAI,

BUDDHA'S OMNISCIENT POWER OF PERCEPTION

IRH Press

Originally published in Japan as
Kanjizairiki - Daiuchu no Jikuukan wo Koete -
by IRH Press Co., Ltd., in June 2020

BOOKS
IRH PRESS
New York

ISBN: 978-1-958655-29-0

Printed in Canada

First Edition

観自在力

KANJIZAI,

BUDDHA'S OMNISCIENT POWER OF PERCEPTION

Going Beyond Time, Space, and the Great Universe

EL CANTARE
RYUHO OKAWA

IRH Press

Contents

Chapter 1

The Great Universe and Human Beings

Chapter 2
The Real Power of Human Beings

Chapter 3

The Basics of Kanjizai

Chapter 4

The Development of Kanjizai

Chapter 5
The Ultimate Form of Kanjizai

Chapter 6

The State of God-as-Self

Chapter 7
A Lecture on *Kanjizai*

PREFACE TO THE NEW AND REVISED EDITION

Following the recent release of the revised and reprinted edition of *Rojin, Buddha's Mystical Power*, I have now revised this book, *Kanjizai, Buddha's Omniscient Power of Perception*, which I wrote at the age of 32, roughly 32 years ago, during the second year of Happy Science. In this edition, I have added Chapter Seven—a secret lecture I gave at the time, exclusively for Happy Science lecturers, to explain the original version of *Kanjizai*.

Both books—*Rojin* and *Kanjizai*—talk extensively about enlightenment, spiritual powers, and the secrets of the higher-dimensional worlds. I stopped printing them at one point because I thought the content was too difficult and unnecessary for the believers, as Happy Science was still in its second year. However, even after I conducted many spiritual messages in front of live audiences in the last 10 years or so, which were published in over 500 books, some people still think of me as a mere channeler (spiritual medium). Others assume, with their shallow thinking, that I am simply putting on an act using my knowledge when giving spiritual messages. For these reasons, I have decided to republish these books to elaborate in a rational way on the extent of my spiritual powers and enlightenment.

When Shakyamuni Buddha attained Great Enlightenment under the bodhi tree nearly 2,600 years ago, he supposedly gained "three insights" (three types of transcendental wisdom). Of course, these insights are spiritual abilities that come with enlightenment. They are: (1) *Shukumyo-myo* (fate-reading), (2) *Tengen-myo* (clairvoyance), and (3) *Rojin-myo* (spiritual wisdom). According to Buddhist dictionaries and other sources, *Shukumyo-myo* is the ability to know your own past lives and those of others, *Tengen-myo* is the ability to see your future lives and those of others, and *Rojin-myo* is the ability to conquer worldly delusions based on the Truth taught by Buddhism and maintain an attachment-free state of mind.

In addition to the three insights, there is also a concept called the Six Divine Supernatural Powers, namely, (1) astral travel, (2) clairvoyance, (3) clairaudience, (4) mind-reading, (5) fate-reading, and (6) Rojin (spiritual wisdom). The fact that these two concepts have three powers in common clearly demonstrates that Shakyamuni Buddha gained mystical spiritual powers when he attained enlightenment. As a religious leader of today, I can declare this to be true.

The closest power to Kanjizai, which is the title of this book, would be *Tengen-myo* of the three insights, or *clairvoyance* of the Six Divine Supernatural Powers. Most

Buddhist scholars know nothing about spiritual abilities, so their explanations are not worth reading. I mainly use *clairvoyance*, *clairaudience*, *mind-reading*, and *fate-reading* of the Six Divine Supernatural Powers to conduct the form of research I call "spiritual reading."

The power of astral travel has to do with astral projection, interdimensional travel, and the enlightenment of "universe-as-self," which is described in this book. The power of mind-reading has to do with the enlightenment of *Nyoshin* (the enlightenment of the seventh and eighth dimensions) and partly with Kanjizai as well. Some scholars explain fate-reading as the ability to know your past lives and clairvoyance as the ability to know your future lives, or the place of your soul's next reincarnation. However, it is better to understand fate-reading as the ability to know your past, present, and future lives, clairvoyance as the power of Kanjizai, and clairaudience as the ability to receive spiritual messages.

If you read Chapters Six and Seven of this book, you will understand that my spiritual powers far surpass those of Shakyamuni Buddha, and that my enlightenment is the highest and the greatest ever in human history.

This book was by no means written to boast my powers. It is meant to serve as a warning to religious people who are at the mercy of superficial spiritual powers.

The last and most victorious Buddha has now appeared and is teaching humankind the Will of God or Buddha. Blessed are those who can believe in this Truth.

Ryuho Okawa
Master & CEO of Happy Science Group
May 11, 2020

PREFACE

This book, *Kanjizai, Buddha's Omniscient Power of Perception*, was written to illustrate the ultimate level of spiritual ability by building on the previously published book, *Rojin, Buddha's Mystical Power.* What makes this book unique is that I have not only explained spiritual powers but have also delved into the secrets of the great universe. I have focused closely on the secrets of the great universe and the existence of God, who can be found at the deepest recesses of the great universe. I believe I have revealed everything I know at this point in time about the views of the universe and of God.

The developmental stages of enlightenment and the understanding of the universe and God described in this book eloquently teach the power of Kanjizai. This spiritual power is extremely high-level, and therefore, humans should not aim to attain it in their spiritual discipline. But after seeing many people become intoxicated by spiritual powers and fall into worshiping them, I believe it is worth showing people the ultimate level of Kanjizai. I hope that this knowledge will serve as a great guide for people to keep advancing in their spiritual learning with humility.

In any case, I am truly happy to be able to publish this book at this point in time.

Ryuho Okawa
Master & CEO of Happy Science Group
September 1988

Chapter 1

The Great Universe and Human Beings

1
Mysteries of the Great Universe

There are many secrets in the great universe

The planet Earth that we live on seems quite mysterious when we look at it from an infinitely distant viewpoint. This is a perspective that extraterrestrial beings have, and as a matter of fact, it is an objective view of the Earth. We who live on the surface of the Earth fail to see its true, genuine nature. We can hardly believe that the Earth is a sphere that rotates on its axis because we, ourselves, do not experience it as reality. It is not easy to understand from our own experience that the Earth, which we live on, rotates on its axis every 24 hours and also orbits the Sun. We just know that a day consists of daytime and nighttime, and it feels as though the stars, the Moon, and the Sun are orbiting around us.

Even the way the planet Earth exists is beyond mysterious to humans, let alone the great universe. We must acknowledge that the great universe contains countless secrets that humans won't possibly understand. When pondering whether humans can ever understand or recognize the true nature of the great universe, I may not be the only one to let out a deep sigh. Indeed, it is incredibly difficult for humans to firmly grasp the nature of the place we live in.

Since we are living in a world that we do not necessarily recognize correctly, it is even more difficult to grasp the nature of the human beings that exist within it. It is similar to the way you can't tell how fast you are really going if you run inside a moving train. For example, if someone runs at a speed of 20 km/h (12 mph) in the same direction as a train that is traveling at 40 km/h (25 mph), they will actually be moving at 60 km/h (37 mph). But to the person running inside the train, it will only feel as though they are moving at 20 km/h (12 mph). In the same way, we can assume that we, who live on the Earth, which is a planet in motion within the great universe, which is also in motion, are different from the way we perceive and recognize ourselves. Here lies the mystery of the great universe. The truth is that people cannot fully grasp the objective picture of the great universe.

Kanjizai bridges the mysteries of the great universe and the true nature of human beings

Now, what if we remove our human perspective and look at the great universe without it? Is it possible to look at the universe from an objective viewpoint? This is beyond human comprehension.

People can only see the universe through their human eyes, but at the same time, the universe seen through human eyes is also a mysterious world. We may be able to accept in our minds that creatures exist in the universe other than the humans living on the Earth, but we would not be so happy if we actually encountered them. This is probably because we fear the unknown. Nevertheless, no matter how you view it, it is far more bizarre and far-fetched to assume that no human-like beings live in this boundlessly great universe other than us earthlings. I am sure you all agree.

In this book, I would like to contemplate the existence of human beings while also keeping the perspective of the great universe in mind. I will talk about Kanjizai as a bridge that connects the mysteries of the great universe and the true nature of human beings. This is the aim of this book.

2
Infinite Wisdom

In actual fact, there is a power that runs throughout the great universe. It has been said since ancient times that God or Buddha is the power that embraces the universe, the wisdom that created it, and the energy that is brimming within it. Then, how can humans understand this infinite wisdom? Is it even possible for us to perceive it?

I would like to give three reasons why we can assume that this infinite wisdom exists.

Reason 1: The universe appears to be sustaining human life

The first reason is the fact that this universe appears to be sustaining human life, at least from the perspective of us humans living on the Earth. When we look at our planet, we can say that humans have been given an appropriate environment to live in. The Earth is a planet with abundant water. About 70 percent of the planet is covered by oceans and seas, and about 30 percent by land. Our planet is indeed blessed with water. On the land, there is plentiful greenery, which provides us with a constant supply of oxygen. There is also sunlight, which is necessary to maintain greenery; plants absorb sunlight to undergo photosynthesis, produce carbohydrates, and release oxygen. This wonderful phenomenon takes place every single day as if it were nothing special.

You all probably learned about photosynthesis in science class, but if you think about it, how could you ever believe that leaves are equipped with these factory-like functions? Isn't it incredible that leaves have manufacturing equipment called chloroplasts that capture sunlight energy to produce carbohydrates and release oxygen at the same time? Could humans ever create anything like it? Even in the 21st century, after there have been tremendous advancements in science, humans are still unable to create chlorophyll. It would be phenomenal if we could invent a device that could produce carbohydrates and oxygen just by having light shone onto it, but that is an impossible reality. As you can see, a process that could never be invented by humans is taking place on Earth naturally every day.

Another amazing fact is that we have a perfect balance of day and night. If the Earth were not a sphere but a flat disc that only ever exposed one side to the Sun, half of the Earth would be a scorching hell, while the other half would be a freezing hell. Both the front and the back sides of the

Earth would become like hell. But the Earth is actually a perfectly-shaped sphere that rotates on its axis, giving us both day and night. As a result, different kinds of creatures can live in all areas of the planet. I sense that great wisdom is at work here, too.

Not only humans, but also many other creatures, such as plants and animals, live on the Earth. This, too, is a truly amazing phenomenon. It means that energy is constantly being provided to support the lives of these creatures. It also means that the Earth is located at an optimal distance from the Sun to receive the appropriate amount of heat. If the Earth were closer to the Sun, it would be too hot for life to exist, and if it were farther away, it would be too cold; but the Earth is located at just the right distance to allow life to exist on it.

From what I have mentioned above, we can see that the Earth is sustaining the lives of many life forms that live on it. This is one of the reasons why we can assume that there is infinite wisdom in the universe.

Reason 2: The existence of gravitational forces

The second reason to believe that the universe is overflowing with infinite wisdom is in the gravitational attraction that exists between stars and planets. This may seem like nothing special, but from an infinitely distant viewpoint, you will notice that the universe is held together by the gravitational force that exists between each star and planet.

The seemingly empty universe is dotted with numerous planets. Each of these planets serves as a nucleus that helps to form the universe. Each planet exerts a gravitational force that attracts other planets, building the framework of the universe, much like how a tent is held up by the poles that support it. This is truly mysterious, but it is the only way to describe the structure of the universe. It is similar to a spider's web, which you have all probably seen in your life. The threads of a spider's web extend outward, like branches, in radial lines from the center, which are then held together with threads that run crosswise, much like the mesh of a fishing net. Likewise, the stars and planets serve as the "knots" that lie at the intersections of the invisible "warp and weft" of the universe. The universe is supported by these celestial bodies. The gravitational forces of these heavenly bodies hold the universe together.

Outer space is an almost boundless world. It does not consist of length, width, and height that humans can see.

What gives the universe structure is gravitational forces, not length, width, or depth. The many stars and planets that exist in the universe have a gravitational force. The sum of these forces keeps the space of the expansive universe limited. If there were no gravitational forces between stars and planets, the universe would expand infinitely and go out of control, but the gravitational forces give the universe a limit.

I have just described stellar dynamics to talk about infinite wisdom. I have explained that the very actions of celestial objects attracting each other under the law of physics determine the shape and the space of the universe. The existence of these gravitational forces is the very reason various objects exist in the universe. You must have heard of black holes that infinitely draw in and swallow everything that comes near them. A black hole is a huge, spherical field with an extremely high gravitational force that even absorbs heat and light. However, this is an exception when it comes to celestial bodies. Usually, stars and planets respond to each other by working to pull each other. This is how the universe maintains itself, which is the basis for various things existing within it.

If the universe were not made up of stars and planets pulling or repelling each other, but instead were made up of black holes that one-sidedly absorb things or a space that only expands infinitely, then there would be no celestial bodies. There would be no Earth, either. This would also mean that no living creatures, including humans and animals, would be able to live in the universe. We would just drift away to a far distant place, as if being thrown out of a spaceship, and would not be able to carry out any activities as living beings. The fact that all kinds of stars and planets exist and are pulling each other to create their own field of activity is the basis for various creatures to live in the universe and for those celestial bodies to function according to their own rules. This is why the Solar System and the Milky Way Galaxy exist as they are. Without these rules, the Milky Way would disperse and the Solar System would dissolve. The fact that our galaxy and the Solar System do not disperse or break apart shows that these creative spaces exist for a reason.

Reason 3: The creation of thermal energy

As the third example of why we can feel infinite wisdom flowing throughout the universe, I would like to bring up the creation of thermal energy. Needless to say, the Sun in our Solar System emits heat energy that all creatures depend on to live, but the Earth is not the only planet that receives sunlight. The truth is that a multitude of suns exist in this great universe, possibly hundreds of billions in our galaxy alone. The very fact that so many suns have been created in different locations implies that they provide energy for many creatures to live. In other words, each sun releases energy to nurture the "created beings" that live in this universe, on behalf of God or Buddha. I believe that the very existence of suns is proof that wisdom is flowing throughout the great universe.

3
The Infinitely Small and the Infinitely Large

There may be a "giant" bigger than the universe

To understand outer space, we need to think about the true meaning of size. In other words, we need to consider *the infinitesimal* and *the infinite.* What defines something as "small" or "large"? For example, even a small puddle or a droplet of water looks as though it contains an infinite universe when observed under an electron microscope. Similarly, this vast universe itself might be like the world under an electron microscope.

Outer space is, indeed, vast and boundless to the human eye. But let's suppose there is a greater being that is far bigger than our universe. How would the universe appear to him? What do you think it would look like? What would you do if a giant existed like the ones in ancient myths, and to him, this universe is like a tiny puddle? What if the universe you thought to be so vast was no bigger than a puddle on the road, and the giant could easily step over it? What if the stars and planets in our universe were no different from water particles inside a puddle? If the giant looked at us human beings, how would we appear to him?

I see a very interesting possibility here. I wonder if anyone can completely deny the existence of this giant. If he does exist, he could write a new version of *Gulliver's Travels* to describe the universe, the Earth, and human beings from his perspective. If I were asked whether there could be a giant bigger than the universe, I would bet on "yes" as the answer because I think that is more logical and likely. I feel that human beings, who are less than about seven feet tall, are too small a scale to use in gauging this vast universe. Perhaps we could use the diameter of this galaxy to do so.

The experience of oneness with the universe

We live in an extremely mysterious world from both the micro and macro perspectives. But how big do the universe, the Earth, and human beings appear from a spiritual perspective? If we assume that a spiritual giant, namely God or Buddha, exists, this universe would probably appear like a small puddle or a baseball in His eyes.

I have mentioned previously that even we, small beings, who are living on this planet, can experience oneness with the universe when we spiritually awaken, attain enlightenment, and become awakened ones. This experience is called the enlightenment of "universe-as-self." This enlightenment consists of roughly two stages. In the first stage, your spiritual body becomes extremely large to the point where you see the Earth far below you. In the second stage, your spiritual body expands as big as the universe, and you become one with the universe. In this second stage, you are approaching the state of "God-as-self," or oneness with God. When we, the souls living on Earth, open our spiritual channel and attain the highest enlightenment, our spiritual bodies and the space within our souls—that is to say, the size of our souls—will expand to the size of the universe.

A soul that resides in a human body that is less than seven feet tall can become as large as the universe. From this, we can assume that the real size of the universe is much smaller than we think. A soul, which is as small as a single point or a tiny dot pricked by the tip of a needle when compared to the size of the universe, can expand infinitely and encompass the universe. The fact that this is possible in itself tells us the real scale of the universe. In other words, it is more logical to assume that there is a Being who is looking at this great universe as if it were a baseball or something in the palm of His hand.

Therefore, this third-dimensional universe is made up of multiple layers. Just as a small puddle—or a mini-universe—that we can see with the naked eye contains a macrocosm under a microscope, our bodies contain a universe of their own. In the same way, we can assume that this universe itself is also one of the elements that make up a greater entity. Thus, we can say that the universe does not consist of fixed measurements of length, width, and height but instead contains multiple layers of universes within it.

4
Humans as Spiritual Beings

Spirits are intellectual energy without form

In the previous section, I talked about the state of "universe-as-self." You can understand this enlightenment to a certain level by reading other books of mine that describe it in different ways. The soul of Shakyamuni Buddha, who was active in India about 2,600 years ago, experienced this enlightenment of "universe-as-self." When he was meditating under the bodhi tree, his spiritual body left his physical body and looked down upon it from far above. He then went higher and looked down upon stars and planets, and eventually reached the end of the great universe. Back then, Shakyamuni Buddha could not explain this spiritual experience or phenomenon theoretically, but I think I can to some extent. It is related to one's recognition of the spirit or the true form of the spirit. I have said again and again that the spirit is energy, or more precisely, intellectual energy without shape or form. But many people still do not seem to understand the true meaning of what I am saying. So now, I would like you to think about exactly what this formless energy is.

Imagine a lighthouse radiating light in the darkness. On a foggy night, you can see that the lighthouse is emitting light because it shows up as a white band reflected on the fog. The part of the light that hits the fog appears to be real, as if a white band exists, but it is merely the water vapor reflecting the light. Human beings, who are defined by their physical bodies, are just like the beam from the lighthouse that hits the fog. The existence of light is proven only when there is something to reflect it. When there is water vapor, we can see the light, but without water vapor, we can hardly see the rotating beam of light.

The life energy that makes up a human is light that comes from far, far away. This colorless, transparent light radiates outward in all directions from an infinitely distant point. This light is neither perceivable nor recognizable on its own. Its existence is defined by way of a material object, in other words, a physical medium, just like in the example of the light reflected by the fog. When the colorless and transparent light passes through a mode of existence, in this case a human body, it appears as though there is a human-sized soul. When it passes through an animal's body, it appears as though a soul is residing in it. After all, what appears as a soul is the Light of God or Buddha that has reflected off a physical object.

Essentially, life energy does not exist as a separate, independent entity; it is a spiritual energy emitted in all directions from an infinitely distant point. When this energy happens to fit into a three-dimensional existence, it appears as though there is an individual life form. In other words, the human souls that we often refer to are not separate from one another, like balls of cotton candy that are made individually. They are actually part of a limitless life energy that takes a particular form when it temporarily passes through a certain object, in the same way that a mold works.

The light that shines forth from an infinite distance not only exists in the third-dimensional space but also exists in the multidimensional space of the fourth dimension and beyond. This means that this light not only flows through space, namely the third dimension consisting of height, length, and width, but also through time. The same light passes through the past, present, and future.

The metaphor of a screen shaped like a human body

Human existence can also be explained in the following way. Imagine light traveling in a straight line. Suppose there are three obstacles, or three films, along its path. Light must pass through the first thin film, then the second, and then the third. What will appear as light passes through each screen? When light passes through the first screen, it shows your past life; when it passes through the second screen, it shows your current life; and when it passes through the third screen, it shows your future life. This is how you can see a human as a spiritual entity.

Let me explain this differently using the same screen metaphor. To make it easier for you to understand, imagine that the screen is shaped like a human body and has its own unique character. Suppose there are no identical human-shaped screens. This means that each of you has your own, unique screen. Let's say you are given three screens—although you actually have four, five, or six of them—that are all lined up. Now, imagine light coming in from an infinitely distant point and passing through the first screen, then the second, and then the third. Although we know that light travels extremely fast, here, let us suppose that light travels at a very slow pace. From the perspective of something that travels faster than light, light will appear to travel very slowly. Perhaps this is the perspective of God or Buddha. So, let us imagine from this point of view.

As light slowly approaches from a distance, it shines on and fills the first human body-shaped screen. The moment the screen emits bright light marks the "first birth." Light then passes through the first screen and moves on to the second screen. The time it takes for light to travel from the first screen to the second is usually a few hundred or a few thousand years. The second screen will shine brilliantly the moment light reaches it. Now, the first and second screens are shining brightly because light has reached both of them, but the third screen and beyond are still not lit. This means that the first and second screens—which are your past life and present life, respectively—have been allowed to exist as human-shaped beings. Once light passes through one of these screens, it then moves onto the "next you," that is, your next life. In this way, what you think of as a single human being is actually one of the manifestations of light that passes through multiple human-shaped screens of the same character, one by one. To put it differently, the character of each human becomes apparent when light, which supposedly travels at a limited speed, passes through the screen.

All of you probably define humans as beings that can be measured with length, width, and height, and as creatures that possess arms, legs, and a head. You probably believe that human beings with such a kind of fixed shape are undergoing reincarnation over and over again. But in truth, if you look at human existence from the perspective of the great universe, it is like the metaphor I have just outlined.

In the explanation above, I took a three-dimensional human being to be a two-dimensional being using the metaphor of a flat, human-shaped screen. If I were to interpret humans in another way, we are also like small light bulbs in an electrical circuit. When an electrical current runs through the circuit of 10 or 20 small light bulbs, each of them lights up one after the other. This illustrates the process of reincarnation of human souls. If we think on a bigger scale and take these light bulbs as stars, we can assume that the light bulbs going on and off represent the birth and death of stars.

Based on what I have explained so far, I would like you to be aware that there could be completely different definitions of a human being from a spiritual perspective. In fact, there is nothing to guarantee that the self-awareness we have is correct. I hope you will always keep this new perspective in mind.

5
Proof that Humans are Children of God or Buddha

The power to overcome and transform environmental factors

I explained human existence using the metaphor of a screen, but are human beings really such motionless existences? When we think more about it, we come to realize that the human-like screens do not lie motionless but are endowed with the ability to move in their own way. Humans are not simply human-shaped molds; while they appear to have a fixed shape, they can also carry out various activities.

Now, let us delve deeper and move on to the next topic. Where does the proof lie that human beings are children of God or Buddha? Human beings are bound by external conditions, such as their environment, but in truth, they have the capability to overcome all of them. I believe this very fact proves that humans are children of God or Buddha.

From the viewpoint of a gigantic being, humans are nothing more than screens through which light passes, or small, stationary light bulbs. But it is also true that these human-shaped screens, or light bulbs, that appear to be stationary can move proactively. Therefore, we can deduce the following truth: "Human beings exist in the infinite expanse of the universe and live through the endless flow of time. They are restricted by the external environment, but even so, they can overcome their environment and proactively transform it. They have the power to do so."

The way each person reflects God's Light differs depending on their effort

Let me elaborate on what I have just said. When the Light of God or Buddha comes from an infinite distance and passes through the first screen, for example, the screen usually shines white. But the way the screen reflects or disperses the light differs depending on the effort made by each screen. To be more specific, the light can appear green when it passes through a particular person's screen, but gold when it passes through someone else's. The light might appear red or purple in other people's cases. Each screen exists in a form that reflects a specific color of light. The secret to manifesting different colors lies in the activity that each screen takes on.

The light is made up of an infinite number of colors within the color spectrum; these colors all mix to make colorless, transparent light. From another point of view, we can see that light is made up of many bundles of colors. If you were to pick out a specific color from those bundles and proactively accept it as your own, your body would emit the light of that color. Similarly, even though the screens are all shaped like a human, each screen has its own tendency when transmitting the light, which means that the screen absorbs certain colors while deflecting others. This unique tendency to reflect or resist certain colors or light explicitly shows each screen's unique character. This is the proactive behavior of human beings.

The intensity of the light passing through the screen changes depending on the screen's ability. From this, we can see that the color and intensity of light can change depending on the efforts that we humans are making. In other words, the proof that humans are children of God or Buddha lies in the very fact that humans can alter the Light emitted by God or Buddha with their own free will and self-help efforts. They can change the way they absorb or reflect that Light and change what it creates.

Then, what is this power that can alter the Light emitted by God? What kind of beings can receive Light from God and determine how to alter it? As a matter of fact, this power itself also comes from God. The power humans have to alter

Light into something of their own making is the same power that God possesses; it is equal in essence, quality, and level to the power of God.

So, this power of humans is an energy generated by the power of God. Therefore, the proof that we humans are children of God or Buddha lies in the fact that we can overcome and change the environmental factors created by Him using our own free will, and that we can express our own unique character. Here lies the reason why humans are considered to be children of God.

6
Secrets of Spiritual Power

All humans are innately endowed with spiritual power

I explained that human beings are children of God or Buddha. In fact, the biggest proof of this is the spiritual power humans have. Spiritual power is difficult to understand for people living on earth. It is a very difficult concept. Because it is thought that ordinary people do not possess spiritual power, people often consider that psychics are very different from them, like aliens from another planet. They tend to think of spiritual power as a dubious sham. But the truth is that spiritual power, itself, reveals the true nature of human beings, which is that they originated from God. Moreover, this very power teaches us the true nature of the soul and the truth that the soul is the essence of a human.

Let me explain it using another example. The physical body is like a silkworm cocoon that has the Light of God or Buddha inside it. The light barely leaks out from the thick layer of the cocoon. Sometimes it grows brighter and sometimes dimmer, like a blinking lamp. When the light gets brighter—in other words, when the Light of God shines brighter—it streaks through the cocoon. You could say that this state, in which the light shines through, is the state of exerting spiritual power while living with a physical body. Everyone certainly possesses this light within, but if it is dim, it will not streak through the cocoon, that is, the physical body. But when the light is amplified beyond the threshold, it will shine through and be exerted as spiritual power. So, we can say that all people are innately endowed with spiritual power. We all have it as hidden potential, but it will not be visible unless something causes us to increase our inner light.

The importance of restoring our power of creativity

Conversely, it is also a fact that the spiritual power of humans who live in this world is limited. Although it is possible for us to emit some light, it is difficult for us to emit the entire light we were originally endowed with. What we emit is merely the light that has leaked through the cocoon, or the physical body. Therefore, humans are not able to emit the original light itself. We are unable to go as far as to show that the soul itself is light.

Let me explain this from another angle. In heaven, or the world of the fourth dimension and beyond, souls emit light according to their spiritual level. Beings that give off a great amount of light are too dazzling for others to see. However, even their bright light dims significantly when they dwell in a cocoon, that is, the physical body. As a result, they are unable to emit their light at its full intensity. I have talked about how souls from different dimensions, ranging from the fourth to the ninth dimension, reincarnate into this earthly world. However, even great beings of light can only emit a small amount of light when they reside in a cocoon. Therefore, we can say that the spiritual powers of psychics living in this world are also limited.

In what sense are their powers limited? Truthfully speaking, they are most limited in their power of creativity. In the world of spirits or souls, we are given the power of creativity that is nearly infinite. This is precisely the power that turns our thoughts into reality. We possess this limitless power. However, once we dwell in a physical body, the power of our creativity weakens significantly. This happens simply because the power of light we have within us is weakened. The secret to developing our spiritual power lies in how we can restore our power of creativity and exert our original strength.

The true meaning of Kanjizai can be grasped by journeying to the other-dimensional world

Through this book, *Kanjizai,* I will explore and investigate the following points: "How can we regain the abilities we have lost and live a life full of radiance? What methods can we use to achieve this? Are there any limitations to the amount of light we can emit?"

In doing so, I do not intend to simply show off the phenomena of the spiritual world that people are often immersed in. Rather, I would like to talk about the power of Kanjizai as a way to objectively study the true nature of human beings and the true nature of the universe.

The power of Kanjizai is akin to the power of God or Buddha. It is the power to see through to the essence of all things, to understand the secrets of this world, and to clearly and vividly grasp everything like God does. To understand the essence of this power, we must go beyond our three-dimensional perception. Only when we set out on a journey to the other-dimensional world can we grasp the true meaning of Kanjizai. Now, let me take you on a long, exciting journey.

Chapter 2

The Real Power of Human Beings

1
True Abilities of Human Beings

Intuition and insight

Chapter One was about the great universe and human beings. In Chapter Two, I would like to talk about the real power or the true potential of human beings. But before delving into the main topic, I must first point out that people are still ignorant of the true, innate abilities of human beings. What this means is that although people are naturally using their innate abilities, many are still unaware of their real potential.

Take intuition, for example. People naturally use their intuition to read other people's thoughts or feelings. This ability is different from logical thinking or physical analysis. The way people understand someone's feelings is not by analyzing them and thinking, "Based on how their facial expression changed, they must be thinking this way." Rather, they intuitively perceive the other person's feelings from a subtle gesture or change in facial expression. This is a type of spiritual ability. So, we can say that everyone has a certain degree of the spiritual ability called "intuition."

In Chapter One, I used the analogy of light contained in a cocoon and explained that, regardless of the amount of light that shines through the cocoon, everyone is endowed with light. The amount of light that streams through differs depending on the thickness of the cocoon and the intensity of the light, but nonetheless, some light always shines through. This light is manifested as a spiritual ability, which is an extra power of human beings. And this is what is known as insight or intuition.

Women's ability to give birth

The ability of women to give birth is another example of spiritual power at work. Childbirth is, of course, the result of physical interaction between a man and a woman, but there is also a significant spiritual process behind it. Many people live without knowing about this.

What exactly is this ability? First, spiritual power is at work at the time of conception, which precedes childbirth. A baby's sex is determined when a sperm fertilizes an egg. This process is actually guided by spiritual power; fertilization is adjusted to fit the gender plan of the child-to-be. Whether the child is born male or female depends on the combination of the sperm and egg, and conception is carried out according to the plan of the child who will be born from the heavenly world. Angels in charge of conception are working to provide spiritual guidance.

I'm sure you have heard of guardian spirits. In addition to them, there are also guiding spirits who guide the process of conception. When women reach the age and can become pregnant, these spirits begin to guide them. They are like obstetricians or gynecologists of the other world; many of them were actually doctors when they lived in this world. There are also higher guiding spirits involved in matters regarding marriage and childbirth who spiritually guide women through the process of pregnancy.

At the time of conception, the egg and sperm fuse to form a zygote, which will repeatedly undergo mitosis until it gradually develops into a human being. After a little over two months, this entity, which is growing to become a human through cell division, will harbor a soul. That is when the soul that was chosen to be the child of the parents will come down from the heavenly world.

When this happens, the woman expecting a baby becomes a kind of "psychic" because what she is doing is housing another soul with a different character in her own body. This is, in a way, the same as a spiritual possession or mediumship. Therefore, it is no exaggeration to say that all women have shaman-like abilities.

Souls that reside in the fetus at this time are different from ordinary human souls living in the other world. A soul that is scheduled to be reborn goes into a preparation period in the heavenly world, which usually takes about two months. During this time, the soul prepares itself to be born as a baby. To explain it visually, the soul confines itself in a small, capsule-like covering and enters a kind of hibernation or sleep state. Then, when the time comes, it is sent from the heavenly world to enter the mother's womb. When the soul enters the mother's womb, it is not yet fully conscious. But as the days pass by and the mother enters her second trimester, the soul begins to develop clearer awareness and starts living its own life in the mother's womb.

As you can see, spiritual ability is very much part of the process of childbirth. So, human beings are familiar with spiritual ability from the beginning of their lives.

Language proficiency and simultaneous interpretation

Humans are born as babies, and they go through various experiences as they grow up. As infants, they begin to develop language skills, but have you ever thought deeply about this process? Why do you think humans can learn to speak?

After all, learning a language involves a kind of intuition. You learn to speak by first copying what others say, and to do so, you need to intuit the meaning of the word. You pick up a word and pronounce it in a situation similar to where you heard it being used. This is how you learn to speak a language. This suggests that language proficiency is also very closely related to spiritual ability. To rephrase it, it would be impossible to learn a language without having some kind of spiritual ability; this includes the ability to guess or infer the meaning of new words so you can learn and understand them. Therefore, you can say that those who are proficient in a language, be it in their native language or a foreign language, are often spiritually awake.

Another ability I would like to mention is so-called simultaneous interpretation. This is another kind of spiritual ability. If you think about it logically, it should be impossible to translate someone else's speech simultaneously. It inevitably takes a certain amount of time for the speaker's words to enter your ears, be transmitted to your brain, and be translated into another language. So, simultaneous interpretation should be practically impossible. However, many simultaneous interpreters can intuitively understand the general idea of what the speaker is going to say as soon as they hear their first word. In this sense, we can say that this skill is also a highly developed spiritual ability.

What is more, simultaneous interpreters are often guided by specific guiding spirits. For example, English interpreters are often guided by British or American spirits, whereas Chinese interpreters are guided by Chinese spirits. As you can see from this, spiritual power is at work when performing simultaneous interpretation.

Foresight

In addition to these spiritual abilities, there is also the ability to foresee the future. Some people can somehow sense what will happen to them in the future. Sometimes they have a premonition and say something like, "I have a hunch that I'm going to fail the exam," "I have a feeling that something bad is going to happen," or "I'm afraid that misfortune will befall my family." Human beings have this kind of ability as well.

Thus, in reality, we are living in this world with various kinds of spiritual abilities. We have more abilities than we think we do. These abilities that are beyond our recognition, in other words, the extra powers that humans manifest, are actually connected to the spiritual world. So, although many people think of psychics as a different species of human, they are wrong. Essentially, we all have the same abilities; it's just that they manifest in different ways.

2
Developing Spiritual Powers

How to bring out the innate brilliance of your soul

I just spoke about how human beings have innate spiritual abilities, and even though everyone has these abilities, the way they manifest or express them differs from person to person. So now, let us think about how we should go about developing them. At this point in time, there are not enough guidebooks on this theme. Some religious groups and various spiritual research groups are trying to develop spiritual powers, but their methods are still at a level that is not refined enough to be studied as academic learning.

The development of spiritual powers is all about bringing out the innate brilliance of your soul, which, as we have discussed, is confined within a "cocoon." There are two main methods to do this. One is to intensify the light or the brilliance of the soul to the point where it shines through the cocoon. The other method is to create a crack in the cocoon surrounding the soul to allow the light to leak through it. If we were to call the former method "internal medicine," we can call the latter method "surgical treatment." Nonetheless, both are methods for bringing out your inner light.

Method 1: Increasing the amount of light in your soul

Let me explain the first method further, and that is, to strengthen the inherent, unique power of your soul. People who are remembered as great figures have the power to influence many people, even if they are not necessarily considered psychics. This is because they possess a great amount of light. The light contained in their "cocoons" is so powerful that it naturally shines through and illuminates those around them.

There have been countless numbers of people in the past who were not necessarily psychics but who exerted significant influence on future generations. Their strong spiritual light that came from their high spiritual level naturally streamed through them and shone upon those around them. In Japan, for example, there are well-known patriots who were active during the Meiji Restoration (in the nineteenth century). The reason their names have been passed down to this day is not simply because of what they said and did. Back in those times, countless patriots strove hard to achieve their goals, but for some reason, only a handful were exceptionally influential. This is because the amount of light stored in their cocoons was unusually large.

In more recent history, we have the well-known Inazo Nitobe, Soseki Natsume, and Yukichi Fukuzawa, who were all very influential and whose portraits have been used on Japanese banknotes. I doubt that any of them were psychic. Even so, why did they earn so much respect from the Japanese people? The answer is because the amount of light stored in their cocoons was immense enough to shine through. Their light was the source of their power to influence and change the general public. This is how they exerted a great impact on society. This is the first method.

Method 2: Opening your spiritual channel by removing the clouds over your mind

The second method is to crack open the "shell," which is the equivalent of opening a spiritual channel that I often talk about. Of course, simply opening a spiritual channel and acquiring psychic powers does not mean that you possess a great consciousness that is of a high spiritual level. People like Inazo Nitobe, Kanzo Uchimura, Yukichi Fukuzawa, Tadao Yanaihara, and Soseki Natsume, some of whom I just mentioned, are at a very high spiritual level even though their spiritual channels were not open. On the other hand, there are also those who—despite not reaching as high a spiritual level as these prominent figures—become so-called psychics because their light leaks through the crack in their cocoons. This is the other way of bringing out your inner light.

Then, how can you create a crack in your cocoon in order to let your spiritual light radiate through it? Just as I have already explained in my book *Rojin, Buddha's Mystical Power* (New York, IRH Press, 2021), you can do this through the method of repentance in Christianity, purification in Japanese Shinto, or self-reflection in Buddhism. In any case, if you calm and purify your mind and clear the clouds, dirt, or dust covering it, then, surprisingly enough, your cocoon will become transparent. In fact, what appears to be a cocoon is nothing but a third-dimensional cover. The way you bring out your inner light can be described as "opening the window" or "making a crack in the shell."

The physical body, which is a material cover, appears to be perfectly solid at first glance, but in reality, it is not. Even though the physical body appears to completely surround the soul in this third dimension, when viewed from the fourth dimension, it actually has an opening that allows any spiritual being to enter and leave freely. So, how can you gain access to this opening that allows free entry and also keep it open? The method to do so is what we call "opening the spiritual channel."

Everyone has this fourth-dimensional, spiritual pathway, but not everyone can access it or keep it open. So, it is important to know how to open the pathway and maintain that state, just like how a canal is maintained to let water flow. The way to do this is to purify the mind and explore Right Mind, which is what I have been teaching.

Recently, various miracles have been occurring around me. Many pure-hearted people have opened their spiritual channels and gained deeper insight. Moreover, an increasing number of people have become spiritually sensitive. Cases like these show that more and more people are gradually gaining access to the fourth-dimensional pathway they innately have and are beginning to use it properly.

Spiritual powers can be developed through specific methods. I will continue to expand on them from different angles, but for now, please know that there are essentially two main methods to develop spiritual powers.

3
The Extent of Spiritual Powers

People often become conceited when they gain spiritual powers

Having touched upon the methods of developing spiritual powers, I must also talk about the extent of these abilities. There is a big difference in how deep they can go. Most people who say they have gained psychic powers only have very small and limited powers in reality. What they can do is make small predictions, like "when the stolen wallet will be discovered," "what is in your wallet," or "whether it will rain or not." Even people with such minor spiritual powers often become popular in this world. However, these kinds of abilities are different from the profound and deep powers that humans inherently have.

Guessing and foretelling minor events is something even non-human spirits can do in the afterlife in the fourth dimension. That is to say that in the other world, even animal spirits can make such small predictions or see mystical entities that living humans cannot. If you are satisfied with a low level of spiritual powers and live as a self-proclaimed psychic, you will end up having a very unfortunate life, and you will have to take full responsibility for that.

In this modern society, spiritual matters are often perceived negatively. One reason for this is that many people who are into spiritual matters go crazy as they experience numerous mysterious phenomena, or they cause people around them to go crazy. Therefore, it is extremely important to know the depth of spiritual powers. When people gain spiritual powers, they tend to become conceited and so overjoyed that they become blind to what is around them. So, it is all the more important to recognize the level of your spiritual powers objectively.

For example, I gave this book the title, *Kanjizai, Buddha's Omniscient Power of Perception*, with the intention of describing how far true Kanjizai can go. By understanding the extent of Kanjizai, one will realize how limited their spiritual powers are. To deepen your spiritual powers and unleash their true potential, you need to have a firm grasp of the world from a spiritual perspective. If you are solely satisfied with just causing spiritual phenomena, you are less likely to evolve spiritually. Rather, you might even regress. There are probably tens of thousands of people who are considered psychics in this world, but those who only care for spiritual phenomena will eventually stop evolving spiritually and often head into a downward slope. This is why you need to know the methods to deepen your spiritual abilities.

Deepen your understanding of the spiritual world

How, then, can you deepen your spiritual powers? First and foremost, you need to know how human beings were created, the purpose of human life, and how the great universe works. You must also know Buddha's Laws that govern the great universe and learn what kind of actions humans are commanded to take and forbidden from taking, based on these Laws. You must be truly aware of these principles before you exert your spiritual powers. Otherwise, you are still very far from mastering these powers. What I am trying to say is that there is a premise to deepen your spiritual powers. Unless you gain the knowledge of the spiritual world on which spiritual powers are based and understand it intellectually, your powers are still premature.

As you get a deeper understanding of the spiritual world, your power of Kanjizai will become purer and more transparent. You must know that the power of Kanjizai is not about simply being able to guess or foretell things. "What kind of world sustains the power of Kanjizai at the core? What kind of world is Kanjizai being used in? What lies at the source of this power? What is the origin of Kanjizai?" Unless you know these things, you cannot say you have fully mastered this power. This can be compared to how a great chef's knife skills are also an artistry. Many people may think that cooking is simply about chopping up meat and vegetables with a knife, but when someone with the mastery of knife skills cooks, they can create a remarkable dish. To reach that level, you need to first study and master several kinds of dishes.

Some of my readers may possess spiritual powers in reality. If you are one of them, I would like you to know that it is extremely important that you gain the correct understanding of the true world, or the world of Buddha's Truth, and to deepen your understanding one by one. Otherwise, your spiritual powers will never be backed by Buddha's Laws in the truest sense. I cannot repeat enough how important this is.

4
The Unique Characteristics of the Third-Dimensional World

Einstein introduced the idea that time and space can be warped

Having said the above, we must now recognize the unique characteristics of the third-dimensional world. This is because we will not understand the true meaning of spiritual abilities unless we detach ourselves from the third-dimensional world and view this world afresh.

Let me explain what I mean by using science as an example. A scientist named Isaac Newton made many discoveries in physics. He discovered gravity by watching an apple fall from a tree and made many other discoveries in the field of mechanics. He then established the laws of physics based on "space" and "time." Newtonian mechanics, otherwise known as classical mechanics, was established based on the idea that space, consisting of length, width, and height, exists under a certain set of rules and that it is fixed.

However, this idea was dismantled by the emergence of Albert Einstein. Einstein asserted that time and space can warp. He introduced a unique worldview that space can distort and that time can expand and contract. Einstein taught that this third-dimensional space, which Newton believed was fixed and unchangeable, is actually extremely unstable and can expand and contract. As a way to understand this unstable world, he introduced the speed of light as the basic standard. In other words, he tried to measure the universe by recognizing the speed of light—which is the fastest possible speed of any object—to be constantly traveling at about 300,000 kilometers per second (186,411 miles per second). This was Einstein's idea.

Observing the third-dimensional world from the standpoint of highest awareness

When you observe the third-dimensional world from the perspective of the speed of light, it will appear distorted. This may also be true when replacing the speed of light with another standard, for example, awareness, which belongs to the world of the mind. There is a tremendous difference in people's level of awareness, but let us take the highest level of awareness to be constant, just like the speed of light. In other words, let us imagine a person with the highest level of Kanjizai a human being can have, and set his level of awareness as the ultimate. Although awareness cannot be measured in the same way as the speed of light, suppose that his speed, expanse, and capacity to comprehend are constant. Can you imagine how the world would appear to him? You can consider his awareness to be very close to that of Buddha or God. If a person with a tremendous power of Kanjizai like him viewed the world, it would appear similar to the world seen from the speed of light. What this means is that he can tell, at a glance, what kinds of events the Earth has experienced in the past and the future events that the Earth is destined to face.

Let us say that this person with a supreme level of awareness can instantly tell what is occurring in the universe, our galaxy, as well as the worlds outside our galaxy. How would our society appear to him? How would the lives of the earthlings seem? How would people's everyday work at their workplace look like? How would people's family life seem? Please think about these things. To him, people's activities and their spaces would all probably look very distorted. The way people are breaking a sweat and working hard at their jobs would appear quite strange to him.

This is the same as space distorting under the constant speed of light, as Einstein put it, unlike in Newtonian mechanics, where space is fixed. This means people on a spaceship traveling at the speed of light will find themselves elongating and shrinking. Time will also expand and contract. In the same way, to someone living with the highest level of awareness, time will expand and contract, and their recognition of space will also differ.

A person with a high level of awareness will be able to instantly accomplish work that many people won't be able to even after spending decades on it. Let us take the pyramids in Egypt as an example. If a modern architect with cutting-edge technology lived in Egypt when the pyramids were constructed, he would probably introduce methods that people back then would have never thought of. He may tell others, "You can build pyramids easily by using this method." Back in those times, it took 40 to 60 years for people to build a pyramid, but if an advanced architect of today were to make it, it would probably be constructed using a completely new method.

In this modern age, people with different kinds of expertise devote themselves to research in science or compete in developing new products at work. But as you can see from the example above, if someone from a society 500 years or even 2,000 years from now came to the present, they would instantly invent or discover something that people today will never even think of in a lifetime.

Psychics with tremendous powers have the same level of judgment as future people

In the above explanations, I have spoken within the axis of time. But in the case of a psychic with tremendous power or the highest level of awareness, they can make the same level of judgment as people from the future would because their soul transcends time. If a person like that exists in modern society, he or she will be able to come up with groundbreaking ideas, just like how modern-day architects would have ideas that those who built the Pyramid of Khufu could never have come up with.

From this, we can say that human activities conducted in third-dimensional space can change freely; they can stretch, contract, distort, expand, or shrink. If that is the case, although people are expected to do a certain amount of work during the eight-hour workday, this premise will collapse. It would become possible to complete a work that normally takes a year to accomplish in just one day.

On another note, what if someone can see the future? In today's society, we sign up for insurance and save up money to cover potential risks, but what if someone who can see the future ran a life insurance or general insurance company? What do you think would happen? By foreseeing the future, this person may only accept those who would never get ill for insurance coverage, and exclude those who will eventually suffer accidents, injuries, or unexpected deaths. Such a company would undoubtedly make huge profits. Something like this could happen.

With the introduction of Einstein's principle that the speed of light is constant, our understanding of time and space has changed. By the same token, if we consider the greatest spiritual powers as constant, human awareness and human activities that take place within the third-dimensional world will appear diverse. Therefore, from the standpoint of a high-level awareness, the third-dimensional world appears very distorted. I just used human abilities as an example, but this is exactly how the world appears from the perspective of Buddha or God. We can say that this is the true nature of the third-dimensional world.

5
The Deciding Factor that Will Help You Transcend the Third-Dimensional World

Key 1: Uncovering the power of faith

Now, how can humans living in the third-dimensional world transcend this world, gain as much correct information as possible, attain greater awareness as possible, and lead a completely new life? In other words, what are the keys to transcending the third-dimensional world? Here, I would like to talk about the two major points.

The first is to uncover what people have referred to as the "power of faith" since ancient times. Jesus said, "Believe, and a path will open," and when a miracle did not occur, he said, "It is because your faith is weak." Jesus preached, "If you can believe, all things are possible," and "If you believe in God and act on it, you have already accomplished it." You must not take these words of Jesus as mere religious commands or a morality tale. When we explore the power of faith from the standpoint of physics, we cannot help but sense the workings of a great rule.

Just like the awareness I talked about earlier, the power of faith has the power to distort the worldly, third-dimensional laws of physics. This is because the power to believe is very akin to the power of Buddha or God. Just imagine how different a bullet train or an airplane would look from the standpoint of the speed of light. Similarly, when you have a strong power of faith, the earthly laws—such as the laws of physics, economics, and physiology—will bend, just like how an iron bar bends like candy under a tremendous force. For example, a person may fall ill as a natural consequence or as an outcome of their lifestyle, but even so, their illness could possibly be cured in an instant. This is an example of how the power of faith can bring change to a third-dimensional phenomenon.

In Europe, there is a miraculous spring known as the Lourdes Spring. There have been many accounts of miracles where people were cured of their illnesses as soon as they immersed themselves in the spring; some were cured of their ailed hands, and some stood up after their legs were miraculously healed. Scientists analyze the Lourdes water and speculate that certain ingredients and factors have a curing effect, but the truth is, what is in the water has nothing to do with the effect. Then, what is necessary for a miracle to occur? It depends on how strongly the person on earth believes that miracles are real, and it also depends on the power of the high spirits and angels who wish to help that person. When the two sides are bridged together, miracles that transcend the third-dimensional world occur.

It is important to know that the power of faith also has physical power and can bend worldly principles and the law of cause and effect. It has such tremendous power. Once we are aware of this, we cannot simply mock faith like how the Japanese proverb goes: "A human being can even have faith in a chopped sardine head (if you have faith, even trivial things will appear sacred)." We must know that the great laws of Buddha or Buddha's physics are at work in this world.

Even in terms of work, how perfectly or successfully a person can accomplish their task will depend on the power of their belief. This power will manifest as self-confidence on a lower level, but on a higher level, it will appear as the power that accords with the Will of God or Buddha. The power that is in tune with the Will of God or Buddha will enable you to make a phenomenal accomplishment.

Therefore, we need to first think about the power of belief. Ultimately, it is to immediately realize your wish, in other words, to close the gap between your current thought and your final goal. In a sense, it has the same effect as transcending time and space.

Space trips have recently been a hot topic of discussion. It is said that traveling through fourth-dimensional space allows you to travel to planets that would otherwise be impossible to get to by traveling through the third-dimensional world or third-dimensional universe. In reality, many space people have been coming to the Earth from other planets, but they do not necessarily come through third-dimensional space. They actually travel through fourth-dimensional space, so they can move through space in an instant. This space travel ability and the power of faith are actually two sides of the same coin. The power that instantly transfers you to your destination is the power of faith. Space people are applying this power in the field of physics; time and space warp under their strong belief. Further scientific explanation for this phenomenon will gradually be revealed in the future. But first, we need to know that we can transcend the third-dimensional world with the power of thought.

I mentioned that space people use the fourth-dimensional world to travel through space and to come to the Earth. I would like to explain the technical details of how to do so in the future, but as a prerequisite, you need to know and firmly believe that it is possible to travel through other-dimensional space. Unless you believe in it, you will never be able to do so. Thus, as the first key to transcending the third-dimensional world, it is necessary to explore the power of faith from the perspective of physics.

Key 2: Understanding the true nature of Light

The second key to transcending the third-dimensional world is to understand the true nature of Light. To put it another way, it is to understand exactly what kind of power Buddha's wisdom has. The first key was about the power of faith, which is the power to change things using the dynamics of thought. In comparison, the second key is not a proactive approach; it is to understand the power of Light that comes from heaven, otherwise called "Other-Power." To give you the conclusion first, both the efforts of seeking the Truth through Self-Power and Other-Power are the keys to transcending the third-dimensional world.

Other-Power definitely exists. In fact, all the wonderful phenomena of this world would not occur without Other-Power. The Light of Other-Power constantly influences this world in various ways. So what should you do to receive its influence? Depending on how much you understand this, the amount of Light you can receive will vary. For instance, guardian and guiding spirits do exist. If you compare the lives of people who live with the wish to receive their power against the lives of others who deny their existence, you will likely see a tremendous difference between them. Once you know of their existence, you can think about how to receive their power. The most precious ideas and methods actually come from them. So, you need to change yourself to be able to communicate with them and receive their advice.

Now, what does it mean to change yourself to become more receptive to their guidance? It means you must tune the wavelengths of your thoughts to those of your guardian and guiding spirits. How can you do so exactly? You need to think like them in your mind and put those thoughts into practice. Simply thinking like them is not enough; it is important to express your thoughts in your words and actions. By doing so, you will be able to live like a high spirit while still being bound by a physical body. As you live your life like a high spirit on earth, your mind will tune to their wavelengths. This theory accords with the fact that the other world is a place where the law of same wavelengths is at work. Only beings of the same wavelength can live together. For this reason, we who live in this world must learn Buddha's Truth and the thoughts of high spirits and think about how to assimilate them and put them into practice.

To sum up, I introduced two ways to transcend the third-dimensional world. The first was: "Be aware of the power of faith and its tangible power. It has the power to bend the third-dimensional principles." The second was: "You have the potential to take on a part of the Will of the Great Universe that is trying to work on you, so think about how you can receive that power." With these two methods, you can free yourself from the constraints of the third-dimensional world.

6
The Real Power of Human Beings

What is true Self-Power?

To conclude this chapter, I would like to think afresh about the real power of human beings. As I observe many people, there is one thing that often disappoints me. It is a fact that many people who come and go in my life are not living wisely. Even though happiness will come to those who live in tune with the Will of God or Buddha, many people ignore it and choose to live recklessly. There is no end to the number of people who willingly "drive their cars" in dangerous ways and in the wrong directions. Whenever I see them, I am struck by curiosity. I wonder why people ignore the splendid roads that are paved before them and instead drive on the mountainous paths or go down into the valley. I find their actions very odd.

People tend to misunderstand the meaning of Self-Power. Self-Power does not mean to live using cheap tricks. It means to exert yourself to the highest degree after knowing all the truths, including the true way of human life, and the secrets of the mechanisms of the universe and the laws that govern it. Some people do not believe in the world beyond the third-dimensional world or pay respect to their fellow human beings living in this world. They have a sense of distrust toward others and live only by trusting themselves. People who think of Self-Power like this will develop a very unhappy view of life.

The true meaning of Self-Power is to find the "roads" that God or Buddha has laid out in all directions and to "drive" on those roads as you live in this earthly world. This is also the secret to "driving safely." Accidents occur to those who misunderstand this and drive in their own way, and go onto the mountainous paths or into the sea.

You will exert real power when you think and act in accordance with divine will

For humans to exert real power, I believe they first need to go onto the roads of God or Buddha. Only when you are on the well-paved roads of the divine can you drive at 100 kilometers or even 120 kilometers per hour (about 60-75 mph) like you would on a highway. You cannot possibly drive at 100 kilometers per hour on a path by the riverbank or a mountain road. I'm sure you would agree.

Choosing the correct path is the starting point of exerting your real power. First, you need to choose a path that is truly right and stick to it persistently. In the meantime, it is essential to make the utmost effort with the spirit of self-help. I believe this is the method of gaining great spiritual abilities.

The reason some people with various spiritual powers encounter misfortune is that they are not following the righteous road that God or Buddha has constructed. Do not think that Self-Power means to live on your own while regarding everyone else as your enemy and that they are evil. Instead, think of it as the act of driving along the single road running in the world created by God or Buddha. As you keep advancing on that road single-heartedly, you will gain great power. When you are driving, you must always remember that you are not simply driving on a road, but you are driving toward your destination for a great purpose. If you fall into the delusion that you are simply enjoying how fast you are going, you will fall from grace and end up being unhappy. As basic knowledge, please know that the power that accords with divine will is the only real power, and that humans can exert real power only when they think and act in accordance with divine will.

Chapter 3

The Basics of Kanjizai

1
What is Kanjizai?

The ability to perceive all things

From this chapter on, I would like to delve deeper into the topic of Kanjizai. First, let me explain what it is. The term Kanjizai is a Japanese translation of the ancient Indian word *Avalokitesvara.* It is often translated as "Kanjizai Bodhisattva" in Japanese, but this does not mean that there is a bodhisattva named "Kanjizai." It simply means that there are high spirits who have attained the state of Kanjizai or gained the power of Kanjizai, and that these high spirits are sometimes born into a human body. Of course, beings known as "angels of light" in the Spirit World all have the power of Kanjizai, but the extent of their abilities differs from angel to angel. So, in this chapter, I would like to think about Kanjizai in the context of the spiritual power possessed by humans living in the earthly world.

It appears that Kanjizai is known to many people as a form of spiritual power, though they do not know exactly what it is. If I were to define Kanjizai, I would say that it is the ability to perceive all things using unworldly senses. What does it mean to "perceive all things"? At a basic level, Kanjizai manifests as a mind-reading ability. With this ability, you know what others are thinking clearly and vividly. It also manifests as the ability to see various spirits in heaven and to clearly understand the lives of high spirits, all while you live in this world. In addition to these abilities, Kanjizai includes the ability to see people's past, present, and future lives.

Kanjizai comes with heightened and broadened awareness

These are some of the typical abilities of Kanjizai, but it is not right to simply understand them as specific abilities. Rather, they are all manifestations of a heightened and broadened awareness.

When you acquire Kanjizai, you develop an extremely high level of awareness; it feels as though you are an eagle in the sky looking down below from an altitude of several thousand feet. One of the characteristics of Kanjizai is this heightened awareness that allows you to look at the world and understand everything from a considerable height.

The other characteristic of Kanjizai is the broadened awareness that allows you to understand a wide range of things. You gain the ability to "hear one, understand ten" (A Japanese phrase that is similar in meaning to the English proverb, "a word to the wise is enough"). When others consult you for life advice, you will be able to understand their entire situation and deduce all the solutions just by listening to a part of their story. You will instantly understand the heart of their problem without hearing the whole story or all the details. This is possible due to your broadened sense of awareness, where you can understand an extremely wide range of things.

This is what I mean when I say that Kanjizai comes with heightened and broadened awareness. Of course, "heightened" is not the only way to describe it; you could also understand it as "deepened" awareness.

The reason Kanjizai exists and how it differs from Rojin

Let me move on to the next point, which is why Kanjizai exists. In fact, this topic is deeply related to how our souls were created. We are currently living in a confined world known as the three-dimensional space consisting of length, width, and height, but in essence, we are beings that transcend time and space. Kanjizai exists as a way to bridge the gap between what we essentially are and our current selves living in a physical body.

Let me also explain the differences between Kanjizai and Rojin. In my recently revised and republished book, *Rojin,*

Buddha's Mystical Power (New York: IRH Press, 2021), I placed great importance on leading a normal, sensible life if you have high levels of spiritual powers. But many people who possess spiritual powers seem to have a hard time understanding how important this is. While Rojin and Kanjizai are both based on highly advanced spiritual powers, they are exerted in different directions. To be more specific, Rojin is a power that is directed inward in that, while you possess highly advanced spiritual power, you are able to contain it within yourself. On the other hand, Kanjizai is a power that is directed outward, in that you have the ability to unleash highly advanced spiritual power. We can say that people with Kanjizai are aiming to develop the ultimate form of spiritual power.

When you possess Rojin, people around you will hardly notice that you have advanced spiritual powers. In contrast, when you possess Kanjizai, you will clearly appear different from ordinary people in this world. You will also get closer to achieving the state of God or Buddha while you are alive. This is similar to attaining the state of Buddhahood in one's lifetime, which has been mentioned in Buddhism since ancient times.

2
The Basic Theory of Kanjizai

A person with Kanjizai can transcend time

I gave an outline of Kanjizai in the previous section, so now, let me move on to explaining the underlying theory of Kanjizai. Kanjizai is based on the idea that there is essentially nothing in this world that can obstruct our view when we perceive through spiritual eyes. For example, when we look at this world with our physical eyes, lots of things around us block our view. When we are inside a house, we cannot see the outside, and then when we are outside, buildings, mountains, and other objects obstruct our view. However, when we perceive things with our spiritual eyes, we can see right through third-dimensional objects as if they do not exist.

In other words, you can say that Kanjizai draws the powers of the fourth dimension and beyond into this third dimension. This means that, when you use Kanjizai, the laws of physics that apply in the world of the fourth dimension and above will start to work in this third-dimensional world.

In fact, someone with Kanjizai can transcend time. For humans living in this earthly world, time seems to be constant and unchangeable; each hour seems to pass consistently.

Because our watches and other people's watches show the same time, we can assume that we are living in the same time and space.

In heaven, on the other hand, there are ancient gods from 2,000 and 3,000 years ago living there. I can talk to them if I want to, and when I do, they appear in their ancient clothing from 3,000 years ago. How should we perceive time when encountering spirits like this? Do you think they appear in the present time looking the same as they did 3,000 years ago? Or do you think they are still living in the times 3,000 years ago, but can send their consciousnesses to manifest in the present? To tell the truth, both of these scenarios are possible. They would be impossible in the earthly world, but are both possible in the Spirit World. In other words, you can live in the past in this very moment, but you can also live in the past and recognize and influence the world that exists thousands of years ahead of you.

Someone with Kanjizai can freely expand and shrink themselves

Ultimately, the following statement can be made:

A new theory of spiritual relativity that debunks the three-dimensional theory of time and space will eventually be established as the basic theory of Kanjizai. This theory of relativity based on spiritual awareness—which is more advanced than Einstein's theories of special relativity and general relativity—precisely indicates what Kanjizai is.

Let me explain this in another way. People usually recognize themselves based on their physical size, such as how tall or heavy they are, and determine their influence and strength based on those factors. However, when you have Kanjizai, you can freely change yourself by expanding or shrinking, which could include becoming gigantic or minuscule. You have the ability to shape-shift at will.

Considering the size of a living human body, you would never believe someone if they say, for example, that they know what is happening on other planets. But what if your spiritual body could expand to the size of the Milky Way Galaxy? Would you still think it is too difficult to see what is happening on other planets? No, it would become a very simple thing to do. Therefore, I would like you to first understand that there are different levels of awareness.

3
The True Nature of Humans

The spiritual world is like a world created by two mirrors

Now, I would like to talk about the true nature of humans. The time has come for us, living humans, to change how we see our real nature. Although we may acknowledge our souls, we tend to do so based on the shape and size of our physical bodies. However, given that souls are essentially meant to enjoy freedom in the fourth-dimensional world and beyond, it is clear that the soul is not something we can measure with our physical senses. In fact, the soul is extremely difficult for us to understand using earthly senses or perception.

Suppose there is a large mirror in front of you and another one behind you. When you look into the mirror in front of you, you can see your reflection in the mirror behind you, and in that mirror behind you, you can see your reflection in the mirror in front of you. Your image continues to be reflected this way in the two mirrors, so you see an infinite series of reflections of yourself. It appears that space with infinite depth unfolds within a single flat mirror. Although the mirror is flat and only consists of length and width, inside it, you see dozens or hundreds of images of yourself as if multiple worlds are overlapping one another. The spiritual world is actually very similar to the world created by these two mirrors, in that a series of more than dozens or hundreds of your selves are lined up there.

Then, how should you understand the reflections of yourself in the mirror? The truth is that they represent your past selves as well as your future selves. This series of past and future selves is continuously reflected in the mirrors in front of you and behind you. From where you stand, all of the reflections in the large mirror behind you are your past selves, whereas the reflections in the mirror in front of you are your future selves. Although you as a soul are simply standing at a single point, your soul is reflected and manifested infinitely and continuously into the future and into the past. This mysterious analogy serves as an important key to understanding the spiritual world. That is, just as you see multiple selves reflected in the two mirrors, the past and future selves of a soul can appear in infinite layers in the spiritual world.

If you lived in a world created by two mirrors like this, how would you recognize yourself? Which reflection of your self in the front mirror is the real you? Or which reflection in the back mirror is the real you? Would you be able to tell? This peculiar, unusual situation unfolds inside the two-dimensional space of the two mirrors, which exists in the three-dimensional space we live in.

Let us apply this analogy to get a better understanding of the spiritual world. Suppose a spirit living in the fourth dimension has a large mirror in front of it and another behind it. If the spirit looked inside the two mirrors, what would appear? In the mirrors in the fourth dimension, the reflections of the spirit appear in three dimensions rather than two dimensions, like they do in the mirrors in the third dimension, where a series of flat images of selves appear. This means that an infinite number of three-dimensional images of the spirit, consisting of length, width, and height, are reflected in the mirrors of the fourth dimension. This is generally what happens when you move up a dimension.

When a spirit of the fourth dimension looks at these three-dimensional images of itself, it will not know which one of them is its real self. This is the mystery of the time and space we live in.

The reason the Primordial Buddha can split Himself into an infinite number of entities

Perhaps you are gradually getting an idea of the secret behind the Genesis of the Universe. It is said that the Primordial Buddha (the Primordial God) created human beings to express a variety of characteristics in an artistic way. In fact, the way humans were created could have been very similar to what we have been describing about how someone's image is reflected in a mirror. For instance, if a spirit living in the fifth dimension were to look at the reflected image of itself in a fifth-dimensional mirror, a four-dimensional copy of itself would manifest. Similarly, if a spirit living in the sixth dimension were to look at the reflected image of itself in a sixth-dimensional mirror, a five-dimensional copy of itself would manifest.

The same is true in higher dimensions. We do not know which dimension the Primordial Buddha belongs to, but let us say that He exists in the twentieth dimension. If He looked at the reflected image of His self in a mirror, a nineteen-dimensional being would appear. Moreover, if this nineteen-dimensional being were to look at the reflected image of its self in a nineteenth-dimensional mirror, an eighteen-dimensional being would appear.

Assuming that God created the universe in this way, we can gradually get a glimpse of a secret of the universe. Based on this assumption, we can say that it is possible for the Original One to split Himself into an infinite number of entities. While the twentieth-dimensional being is originally a single entity, He can manifest Himself as an infinite number of entities into the past and the future by placing "two large mirrors" in front of and behind Him. The reflections of this twentieth-dimensional being will manifest as countless numbers of nineteen-dimensional beings—in fact, there will be an infinite number. What is more, each image reflected in the mirrors is a separate and independent entity. If we recognize that each of these images has its own unique character, we can then say that each of these nineteen-dimensional entities can reflect images of themselves using nineteenth-dimensional mirrors and produce eighteen-dimensional images. Each of these eighteen-dimensional images can then use eighteenth-dimensional mirrors to create an infinite number of seventeen-dimensional versions of itself. If we assume that each of the dimensions, down to the third dimension, was created in this way, it gives us a clue as to how the Original One was able to express Himself into an infinite number of souls with individual characteristics by projecting and reflecting Himself.

Now, if the being of the twentieth dimension reflects Himself in the mirrors to project His image into the nineteenth, eighteenth, seventeenth..., then tenth... onto fifth, fourth, and third dimensions, what would be the difference between the final forms that were created and the original twentieth-dimensional being? Through countless reflections, what was originally a single existence has split itself into an infinite number of entities, or an infinite number of copies. In other words, an infinite number of entities were created in the image of the Primordial Buddha, but each of them is expressed in a completely different form. While they may all look similar, the way they express themselves varies from entity to entity. This is how the world unfolds.

Humans always try to "gauge" the universe, high spirits, and even God or Buddha based on their own physical size or height and weight, but we also need to consider how we are viewed from their perspective. From their viewpoint, each human being is just one of an infinite number of reflections in a mirror. From this, we can say that the real world is a truly mysterious world.

If God or Buddha were to close the mirrors in the fourth dimension, what would happen to humans in the third dimension? Since the third dimension is a projection of the fourth dimension, closing the fourth-dimensional mirrors would cause the third dimension to disappear, which means humans would also cease to exist or vanish. Likewise, if the mirrors in the fifth dimension were closed, like folding a mirror on a dressing table, the human spirits in the space of the fourth dimension would vanish.

Given all of this, we could say that God or Buddha created living beings in different dimensions by "opening the mirrors."

4
The Ability to See through the Past, the Present, and the Future

The human soul is a series of "selves" continuing from the past into the future

Next, let us consider the ability to see through the three times—the past, present, and future lives of people, which is one of the basic abilities of Kanjizai. This ability enables you to see the past, the present, and the future. You will be able to see what you did in your past lives and what others did in their past lives. You will also be able to see the kind of spiritual ties that a particular person had in their past life that led them to be born into their present life, as well as what kinds of future lives await them.

Shakyamuni Buddha often talked to his disciples about how he could see through their three times. He told them things like, "This is the work you did in your past lives," "You are a religious practitioner in this life because you accumulated good deeds in your past life," or "You shall become a great tathagata in a hundred million years if you start making this kind of effort in this lifetime." Leaving aside the question of how accurately Shakyamuni Buddha was able to see the three times of a person, it is indeed possible to see through someone's past, present, and future lives in the way that he did.

The fact that you are living in the present time indicates you have lived through an infinite past. You would not be who you are now if it weren't for all your past *yous*. Imagine the Japanese cylindrical candy called *Kintaro-ame*. It shows the face of a young Japanese folk hero named Kintaro, no matter where you cut it. If we were to compare humans to this candy, our usual self-recognition would be a flat, two-dimensional image of Kintaro on a cross-section of the candy. But in reality, we are a full stick of candy with a continuous pattern. So, it is essential for those who think of themselves as "a plane surface with length and width only" to be able to recognize themselves as "a long, Kintaro-candy-like existence."

From the perspective of someone with the ability of Kanjizai, a person born into a physical body in this life looks like a single cross-section of a long piece of Kintaro candy. Because they view from a level that is one dimension higher

A traditional Japanese candy called *Kintaro-ame.*

than that of ordinary human beings, they can recognize not only the two-dimensional flat image of Kintaro, but also the thickness of the candy that continues behind it. What's more, they can tell what kind of image will appear depending on the point and the way the candy is cut. On the other hand, those living in the same two-dimensional flat world can only recognize others as a flat, picture-like existence. From this analogy, I hope you can understand what it means to see through the three times of people.

I have just explained the true nature of the soul in the context of a two-dimensional world to make it easier to understand for all of you living in the three-dimensional world. Please know that your life, or your soul, is like a long piece of Kintaro candy that continues from the infinite past into the infinite future. Each incarnation is represented by the cross-section that will appear if the Kintaro candy is cut.

Perhaps some people understand reincarnation as a repeating cycle, but the truth is that it is like cutting an infinitely long piece of Kintaro candy at different points. Our lives go on eternally like a long piece of candy. If the candy is cut at a point that indicates 800 years ago and then again at a point that indicates the present time, for example, it means you were reborn into this world after 800 years. Therefore, you can say that reincarnation simply refers to the point where the candy is cut to expose Kintaro's face.

Human life forms appear differently depending on the viewer's level of awareness

If someone is capable of looking at these "Kintaro candies" from above using their highly advanced spiritual powers, they will be able to tell at a glance what kind of past and future lives each piece of "candy" has. I hope you understand what I mean by this analogy. I am trying to explain what a three-dimensional human is by describing it in the context of a two-dimensional being.

Suppose there are humans living in a two-dimensional space. How would they appear? They would be like paper dolls. I am sure that some of you have played the game called *kamizumo* (paper sumo), where two paper sumo wrestlers have a match on a wrestling ring made out of something like an empty cardboard box. The two players tap on the box on opposite sides to move the paper sumo wrestlers until one of

Paper sumo wrestlers and a ring used in a Japanese game called *kamizumo*.

them falls over. This is how humans would appear in a two-dimensional space; we would be like "paper humans."

As I have mentioned, those in two-dimensional space can only recognize others as a "flat cross-section of a Kintaro candy." However, those living in three-dimensional space have a different perspective from those in two-dimensional space; not only can they see the flat cross-sections, they can also see the entire length of the Kintaro candy. In the third dimension, the soul or life form appears to be like a Kintaro-candy that stretches from the infinite past into the infinite future. Despite so, those in even higher dimensions don't necessarily perceive these souls as the same, long, tube-like entity. From the perspective of a higher dimension, the tube-shaped Kintaro candy—which continues from the infinite past to the infinite future—could look like a doughnut. What you thought was an infinitely long, straight line might be curved like a doughnut when viewed from a higher dimension.

Further, when those in an even higher dimension look at a soul, the doughnut-shaped life form may look like a perfectly round sphere. Perhaps from a dimension even beyond that, it may no longer look like a sphere but more like a single dot or segment of a line. As you can see, there are diverse perspectives depending on the person's level of awareness. I would like you to understand that these differences exist.

Ultimately, seeing through the three times—past, present, and future lives of people—means perceiving the whole picture from a higher dimension, rather than looking at them from the same dimension.

5
Going beyond Time and Space

The universe from the perspective of higher dimensions

So far, I have described various levels of awareness according to the different dimensions. Now, I would like to conclude this chapter by talking about going beyond time and space. We tend to view the world based on space—which has length, width, and height—and time, which flows through space. However, as you can see from the analogy I used in the previous section, something that can only be perceived as a flat image in a particular dimension can be seen as an infinitely stretched tube from a higher dimension, and from an even higher dimension, it appears as a doughnut shape. Moreover, from yet an even higher dimension, it appears as a sphere and, from a dimension above that, it appears as a segment of a line or a single dot. If that is the case, what would the Earth, its inhabitants, the Milky Way Galaxy, and the third-dimensional universe look like from the perspective of much higher dimensions?

I have already revealed that the most highly evolved human spirits reside in the ninth dimension and that planetary consciousnesses exist in the tenth dimension. I have also revealed that stellar consciousnesses of fixed stars like the Sun exist in the eleventh dimension, galactic or star cluster consciousnesses exist in the twelfth dimension, and cosmic consciousnesses exist in the thirteenth dimension.

The great universe as seen from the worlds of the tenth dimension and higher

Then, the next question is how this great universe appears to the consciousnesses in each of these dimensions. Let me first describe how the universe and the Earth look from the perspective of the tenth-dimensional consciousnesses. In fact, the tenth-dimensional planetary consciousnesses see the universe in the same way humans see schools.

I do not know what kind of school you attended as a student, but let me use a four-story reinforced concrete building with dozens of classrooms to illustrate this. Planetary consciousnesses see the galaxy or the universe as if it were a school with different classrooms, with each having a homeroom teacher and a few dozen students. In this analogy, the teachers correspond to the planetary consciousnesses and the students to the consciousnesses of the high spirits, who have developed to the highest degree possible as human spirits. This is the level of recognition the planetary consciousnesses have.

Then, how does this universe appear in the eyes of eleventh-dimensional stellar consciousnesses? The stellar consciousnesses have a slightly higher level of awareness than that of the tenth-dimensional consciousnesses. Drawing on the previous analogy of the school, these stellar consciousnesses do not oversee individual classes but oversee each grade. For example, imagine them supervising 10 classes at the first-grade level or 15 classes at the sixth-grade level. They perceive the universe in this way.

The twelfth-dimensional galactic consciousnesses have a level of awareness similar to that of a school principal. They are in charge of the entire school. Then, what about the thirteenth-dimensional cosmic consciousnesses? They are much like the Minister of Education, Culture, Sports, Science and Technology of Japan, who supervises thousands of schools; they oversee all of the schools. This is how the universe appears in their eyes.

From the perspective of higher-dimensional spirits, the universe does not appear to be something that spreads out infinitely before their eyes but instead a single, compact entity. Although I can only describe it metaphorically now, this is how the universe appears to them.

Let us go even further. How would this third-dimensional universe appear in the eyes of a fourteenth-dimensional existence? It would probably look like a miniature garden or a fishbowl. The fact is that, from the viewpoint of fourteenth-dimensional consciousnesses, the great universe we live in now appears as a floating soap bubble or water droplet. What is more, there is not just one, but two, three, four, or even more droplets that are floating.

This shows the ultimate level of Kanjizai: a power that allows you to go far beyond time and space.

Chapter 4

The Development of Kanjizai

1
Kanjizai and Enlightenment

The power of Kanjizai and a person's enlightenment are directly proportional

In the previous chapter, I talked about the basic theory of Kanjizai. Now, I would like to delve into the main aspect of Kanjizai and explain the relationship between the power of Kanjizai and spiritual abilities.

I will start by discussing whether there is any correlation between enlightenment and Kanjizai. In conclusion, they are closely related to each other as a matter of course. In the Real World, a person's power of Kanjizai develops in direct proportion to their level of enlightenment. However, this may not necessarily be the case in the third-dimensional world. This is because each person is born into this world with a specific mission to fulfill, and they exert their spiritual powers in a way that is most appropriate to achieving that mission. Nevertheless, essentially, a person's power of Kanjizai corresponds to his or her level of enlightenment.

Kanjizai is an extremely developed form of spiritual ability. In this chapter, I would like to talk about how much it relates to enlightenment and how much it manifests as evidence of having attained enlightenment.

It is very difficult for living humans to judge whether or not they have attained enlightenment. Zen Buddhism focuses on attaining enlightenment through meditation, but it is doubtful whether Zen enlightenment is truly accompanied by the power of Kanjizai.

The reason enlightenment enables you to clearly understand other people's feelings

So, what exactly is it about Kanjizai that is closely related to enlightenment? I would say that you cannot exert the power of Kanjizai unless your enlightenment is at least accompanied by some kind of spiritual phenomena or spiritual power. However, you do not need any spiritual powers to manifest the initial stage of Kanjizai. That is because, when you have attained a high level of enlightenment or reached an advanced state of enlightenment, you are able to easily and vividly understand other people's feelings.

Why is it possible for a highly enlightened person to understand other people's feelings? There are two reasons for this. The first is that their state of mind has become so elevated that they can understand the feelings of those who have yet to reach that level. It is similar to climbing a mountain; as you get closer to the summit and look back at the people behind you, you get a clear view of them. This state, where you can clearly see and understand other people, is a power of Kanjizai that comes with a heightened level of awareness.

The other reason is that the person's mind has become so pure and clear that it serves as a kind of mirror, reflecting any distortions that exist in other people's minds. People with perverse thoughts cannot bear to stand before someone in an advanced state of enlightenment. They will generally feel extremely anxious, much like how pigs or sheep feel as they are dragged to a slaughterhouse. As a person's state of enlightenment advances, their mind becomes clearer, and their "polished mirror of the mind" reflects other people's minds very vividly. If you are with someone like this and the reflected image of your mind is well-balanced, you will feel at ease, but if the image of yourself is distorted, you will likely be upset. Most people feel this way. On a fundamental level, human beings are honest with themselves and wish to be good. However, even if they are vaguely aware that they are doing something wrong or living with bad thoughts, when their true colors are shown to them accurately and in a straightforward way, most people end up feeling depressed.

Thus, when you reach a certain level of enlightenment, you acquire the ability to understand others well and to help them realize where they have gone wrong. Although these abilities cannot exactly be called spiritual powers, they are somewhat similar to the power of Kanjizai.

This is one example that shows how enlightenment and Kanjizai are related to each other. In the next section, I would like to talk about how Kanjizai corresponds to each developmental stage of enlightenment.

2
Kanjizai and the Developmental Stages of Enlightenment

Kanjizai and the state of arhat

The state I mentioned in the previous section—where you can get a good understanding of other people's feelings and where your mind has become so clear that it serves as a mirror to reflect the clouded minds of others—is called the enlightenment of arhat in the developmental stages of enlightenment. I often teach that this state of mind corresponds to the upper level of the sixth dimensional Light Realm and is the gateway to entering the world of bodhisattvas in the seventh dimension and beyond.

It is often said that Zen enlightenment—which does not seem to be accompanied by any spiritual powers—corresponds to the enlightenment of arhat. However, some Zen masters were originally spirits from higher spiritual realms and were able to attain the enlightenment of tathagata (of the eighth dimension). For example, Zen master Mumon (Wumen Huikai) was one, and so was Zen master Hakuin, although he was not quite a tathagata but a brahma (of the realm between the seventh and eighth dimensions). These monks attained very high levels of enlightenment by mastering Zen meditation. This is most probably because they had a desire to save the people of the world far and wide, rather than just focusing on their own enlightenment.

Kanjizai and the state of bodhisattva

I described the enlightenment of arhat as a state in which you can understand the feelings of others extensively, and your clear mind acts as a mirror to reflect people's clouded minds. Then, what kinds of abilities will you have when you reach the next stage—the state of bodhisattva? In terms of spiritual abilities, there is not such a great difference between arhats and bodhisattvas. Some people who have attained the state of bodhisattva do not possess any spiritual powers. However, they do possess sharper insight and a very strong power of influence as human beings.

Now, let's think about someone at the level of bodhisattva who gains spiritual powers while they are still alive. How are they different compared to someone at the level of arhat? Frankly speaking, the ultimate difference between arhats and bodhisattvas is that bodhisattvas can understand not only other people's feelings but also the feelings of the masses;

they have a keen sense for the thoughts and feelings of a great number of people.

This is possible because the love of a bodhisattva is not merely a form of self-love, but a love for many people. The love they have for a great number of people is rooted in the care they have for countless people. The point is that their insight and observation do not simply extend to just one or two people but extend to large numbers of people. This means that their everyday concerns are about how to save as many people as possible. For this reason, those who have attained the state of bodhisattva also feel great sorrow. What this means is that they do not just feel their own sadness, but they feel the sadness of many people as their own; in other words, they have great compassion for all kinds of people. This is the state of bodhisattva.

Like bodhisattvas, arhats can also understand the feelings of others. So, in terms of spiritual ability, there isn't a significant difference between bodhisattvas and arhats, except that bodhisattvas are more consistent in their abilities. However, there is a big difference between the two in that bodhisattvas are able to have a caring heart for all kinds of thoughts and concerns of a great number of people.

Kanjizai and the state of brahma

When a person's state of bodhisattva develops further, they eventually reach the highest level of the Bodhisattva Realm called the Brahma Realm, which extends across the seventh and eighth dimensions. Brahmas in both the seventh and eighth dimensions are elementary-level tathagatas, but in terms of their work, they have different missions. Those who reside in the seventh dimension are essentially at the spiritual level of tathagatas but take on the work of bodhisattvas. In contrast, brahmas who reside in the eighth dimension are like the "novices of tathagathas" who are undergoing spiritual training to reach excellence.

We can say that, in general, those at the level of brahma, namely the highest level of bodhisattvas, start to possess Kanjizai, that is, spiritual powers that correspond to higher levels of enlightenment. The brahmas residing in the seventh dimension, who are essentially tathagatas but are working as bodhisattvas possess Kanjizai in a limited sense.

Now, how extensive is a brahma's scope of understanding? Of course, I cannot make a sweeping statement because some of them living as humans in this world have other missions to fulfill and do not possess spiritual powers. So, instead, let us focus our discussion on a specific aspect of Kanjizai: When someone with the enlightenment of a brahma or a high spiritual level possesses spiritual power, to what extent can they perceive things?

First, it goes without saying that they can understand other people's feelings. But what is unique about brahmas is that they can understand a wider range of things, including the feelings of people in distant places and the past lives of other people to a certain extent. It is also from this level that transcendental wisdom, which is wisdom acquired from your past lives, really begins to work. This wisdom is called "Prajnaparamita." It means that, when you reach the state of brahma, you can use the power you have accumulated in your past lives to a considerable degree.

In comparison, arhats still cannot fully use the knowledge they accumulated in their past lives. Although arhats may be able to spiritually demonstrate that they can speak the language of their past lives, they have yet to reach a level where they can use the knowledge they have accumulated in their past lives at will. Compared to brahmas, they only have a vague understanding of their past lives and future lives, or those of others.

Therefore, the full-fledged spiritual power that can be considered Kanjizai begins to manifest from the highest level of the Bodhisattva Realm. In a way, this is the kind of power that reminds you of God.

Kanjizai and the state of tathagata

When you advance further and enter the world of tathagata, you reach the state called *Nyoshin.* Essentially, the state of Nyoshin corresponds to the state of tathagata, but its entry-level abilities can be observed in the world of bodhisattva as well.

How should we understand Nyoshin? It is a state in which you are able to know various things intimately without even having to be there in the present time. This ability is slightly higher than the restricted Kanjizai of brahma. For example: a person who has reached the state of Nyoshin is able to perceive someone living in America while being in Japan; perceive an event that happened thousands of years ago; or perceive several or dozens of someone's past lives the moment they meet him or her.

Thus, the state of Nyoshin enables a person to understand many things without being in the same place at the same time. This is also a manifestation of Kanjizai, and people who reach this state will feel this ability getting very strong.

Kanjizai and the state of ninth-dimensional spirits

Above the state of tathagata is the enlightenment of the ninth dimension. I will explain this again later in the section about the state of *universe-as-self.* This is the state of those who have the highest level of spiritual ability that human beings can possess. To explain it more clearly, these spiritual abilities are not limited to understanding people but also enable you to connect directly to God. When you are in the state of Nyoshin, you already have the ability to be in tune with high spirits. But when you have the ability of the state of Nyoshin of ninth-dimensional spirits, or the ability of the state of universe-as-self, you will be able to directly receive the Will of God.

Having said this, even ninth-dimensional spirits did not always possess great spiritual powers when they lived in a physical body. This was because it was not necessary for some of them to use these powers, like Newton, the scientist. For people like him, the powers remain hidden within. But it would be a lie to say that Newton did not possess any spiritual powers because he could never have come up with so many inventions and discoveries without the support of the heavenly world. He must have been capable of receiving spiritual guidance. Confucius, who is also a ninth-dimensional spirit, did not need to develop or use his spiritual powers to the maximum level because he preached through academic studies. That being said, Confucius did possess the power of Kanjizai, in a sense, because he supposedly saw through people with his extremely sharp eyes. If he didn't, he could not have lived as such an outstanding educator.

I have briefly described how the stages of enlightenment correspond to Kanjizai. I intend to discuss this in more detail in Chapter Six.

3
Kanjizai and Clairvoyance

Next, I would like to talk about Kanjizai and clairvoyance. Many people probably know that clairvoyance is one of the unique senses that psychics have. In general, clairvoyance is the ability to see spirits or scenery in the Spirit World that cannot be perceived with physical eyes; sometimes, it is possible to witness scenes from the past or the future as well. In this sense, Kanjizai is related to clairvoyance.

However, the ability of clairvoyance is not the same as Kanjizai. Clairvoyance is simply the ability to perceive spiritual matters through the physical organ of the eye. When you begin to fully exert the power of Kanjizai, you will realize that perceiving spiritual matters through the physical eye is quite an immature level of ability. The fact that you still need to rely on the senses of your eyes means that your spiritual ability is still insufficient. Since you can only recognize spiritual matters by translating them into third-dimensional concepts, it shows you are still at the beginner stage. When you start to exert the true power of Kanjizai, you will instantly be able to grasp the full picture and essence of things directly and intuitively, as if they are in the palm of your hands, rather than just perceiving them visually.

Suppose you are asked whether the spirit of someone's ancestor is lost. If you possess clairvoyance, you will try to see the spirit visually. However, if you possess Kanjizai, you will instantly know where the spirit is and the situation it is in. You will grasp these things instantly rather than merely perceiving them visually or auditorily. You will not need to use your sense of taste or touch, either. You will just grasp them in a way that is similar to so-called telepathic transmission. This is the difference between clairvoyance and Kanjizai.

Therefore, as your power of Kanjizai develops, you will no longer see spiritually with your two eyes but grasp things as if through a third sensory organ. It feels similar to perceiving things with the third eye. Much like how snails have tentacles, you will have an antenna that can stretch out infinitely to distant places and perceive many things. When your clairvoyance heightens to the level of Kanjizai, you no longer perceive things like scenery in a visual form but grasp them in a more condensed and comprehensive way.

4
Kanjizai and Fate

Is fate predetermined?

I will now move on to the topic of Kanjizai and fate. It is often said that humans have fate and that each person bears their own destiny. The fate of humans has been a topic depicted in various plays and works of literature since the time of Shakespeare. Sometimes, people may face tragedies that are completely beyond human understanding, and at other times, they lead incredibly comical lives. Human life can be like a piece of fabric woven by the threads of fate.

So, how is Kanjizai related to fate? Is it possible to see people's fate with the power of Kanjizai? To answer these questions, I need to touch on how fate is determined. We need to consider how fate is shaped and how we should understand it. The main question is, "Is fate predetermined?" The only answer I can give at this time is, "It is and it is not." This is the truth. The reason I say this is that different conclusions can be drawn depending on the position of the person who is looking at fate.

Can the ultimate God see fate? The answer is, of course, He can. The ultimate God, or the Creator of the Universe, can surely see the future of a single human being. But what about the high spirits who are close to God? How far can they perceive people's fate using their spiritual powers? It depends somewhat on the level of the high spirit, and how accurately each of them can see the future varies as well.

When considering fate as an expedient means to guide people, I am unsure whether it is good to completely reveal a person's fate. For example, what if a baby were born with their life plan in their right hand? What would you think? What would you do if you opened a baby's hand and found his or her life plan written on the palm of their hand? This may be interesting in a way, but it could also be a little disappointing. Parents find joy in raising a newborn baby. It is precisely because they do not know how the baby will turn out that they invest 20 years raising and nurturing the child. All parents have high hopes for their children, but the results will differ depending on the child. If their future was predetermined at birth, their parents would face a different kind of challenge in raising them.

It has been said since ancient times that a person's fate is written in their palm lines. People who study palmistry believe that they can tell a person's fate to a certain extent by reading their palm lines. Even if that is true, palmistry is too vague to predict a person's entire life. In a way, you could say that fate is similar to how it is symbolized by palm lines. The general tendency of a person's fate can be clear to a palm reader with a certain level of expertise, but life is not so simple that it can be written in the palm lines of your hand; reading them won't tell you everything. Palm lines do not tell you the name of the person you are going to marry, nor do they tell you the kind of business you are suited for, or the name of the company you are going to work for. Even so, professional palm readers can generally tell your personality, as well as your fortune when it comes to success, wealth, and good health. The spirits in the Real World can also tell what your general fate is with a relatively high level of accuracy. This means that some courses of your life have already been set.

In a way, Kanjizai is akin to the ability to read palm lines. You may be able to see the course of a person's life, but how it is interpreted will depend on the ability of each person.

To what extent can high spirits see a person's fate?

Then, to what extent can high spirits see a person's fate? Take, for example, the spirits in the Brahma Realm. As far as I know, they can understand 70 to 75 percent of a person's fate using their power of Kanjizai. When it comes to the tathagata class, they can understand up to 80 to 85 percent, and as for the ninth-dimensional spirits, they can understand up to 90 percent of a person's fate. But even for the ninth-dimensional spirits, the remaining 10 percent is left unknown.

Interestingly, the reason for this is that "the person looking at someone's fate" and "the very person living this fate as the protagonist of their life" are not living separately but are connected. As strange as it may sound, the theory of relativity applies here, too, in that someone in motion cannot accurately measure the speed of a moving object. Imagine that you are in a car moving at 100 km/h (about 60 mph), looking at a bullet train moving in the same direction at 200 km/h (about 120 mph). To you, the train will only appear to be moving at 100 km/h. However, if you look at it from a car moving at 100 km/h in the opposite direction, the train will appear to be traveling at 300 km/h (about 180 mph). Similarly, a spirit observing the fate of others is also in the great flow of fate governed by God. In other words, just as I have spoken about the theory of relativity earlier, even high spirits are in the palm of God's hand like His puppets. Just as it is impossible for you to accurately measure the speed of something unless you are completely still, high spirits cannot fully see the fate of someone on earth because they, themselves, are also subject to fate.

So, why does the world function like this? Let me give you an answer to this question by giving you a conclusion. Think about whether there would be any meaning to the work of bodhisattvas if fate were predetermined and unchangeable. The work of bodhisattvas is the act of serving others, giving love, being merciful to others, and helping people to be good and get back on their feet. But if fate were already determined, what could bodhisattvas do for others? It would be the same as Calvin's theory of predestination, which says that those who are meant to be saved have been destined for salvation from the beginning, and those who are not meant to be saved are destined for damnation.

When considering this, we have to note that the idea of predestination strays a little from how high spirits actually think. High spirits do not go and help people by checking them off a list of "To be saved" and "Not to be saved." They do not decide who to save based on a list like this. The reality is that they are filled with the desire to save as many people as possible. But in practice, they can save some, but cannot save others. This is what I mean by the metaphor of someone in a moving car observing a moving bullet train. I am saying that the high spirits who are watching the fate of human beings are also in the palms of God's hands and therefore in the flow of fate governed by God. They, too, are living their fate of saving people and doing the work of a bodhisattva, while at the same time looking at the people going through the ups and downs of life within the flow of their own fate.

From this, we can say that even high spirits view the world and fate in different ways depending on their state of mind. How would high spirits filled with a strong passion to save every single person on earth see people's fate? They would probably think that everyone has the potential to be saved. But some high spirits may think, "I want to save the ones that I find are worthy. I don't really care about the others." When these spirits look at people living in this earthly world, they will probably only focus on saving particular types of people and not pay much attention to others. As you can see, there are difficult aspects to what is called "destiny" or "fate" and the question of whether it is predetermined or not. However, when the ultimate God overviews the situation by looking at the kinds of high spirits that are working, the kinds of actions they are willing to take, and how many people are actually lost, He will likely have a rough idea of how things will turn out in the end. We need to be well aware of these aspects of fate.

5
The Limitations of Human Beings

It is difficult for humans on earth to understand the high-dimensional worlds

So far, I have talked about the development of Kanjizai in various ways, but there is one last thing I must add. It is about our limitations as human beings. Although I have analyzed and explained spiritual abilities in various ways, as long as we, the speaker and the listener, are living as human beings, there will always be some limitations. This is because it is impossible to fully understand spiritual abilities as long as we are living as humans.

Why is that so? As people currently living in the third-dimensional world, the extent to which ordinary humans can understand spiritual matters is limited to around the fourth dimension. In fact, rather than fully understanding it, they can only assume what is going on there. Further, they can only do this with respect to the world that is one dimension above the one they belong to. This means that it is impossible for ordinary humans in the third-dimensional world to even guess what is going on in the world of the sixth dimension and above, such as the seventh dimension, the eighth dimension, and the ninth dimension.

Therefore, it is extremely difficult to explain in third-dimensional terms how the inhabitants of these higher dimensions perceive things or, in other words, the extent of their power of Kanjizai, and how they exert that power. After all, you cannot understand worlds that you have no interest in.

What is necessary to develop the power of Kanjizai to the highest level

Suppose you are interested in baseball and you spend all day practicing it. Those who do not really care about the ball itself will not think any more about it. However, those who are interested in the ball and always analyzing its interior may think about the different ways the ball bounces when they hit it. Some may even tear open a damaged ball to examine the thread and other stuffing inside it. If they gain spiritual powers, they will probably be able to see through the ball without opening it. But if you are not interested in something like this, you probably won't see through the ball even if you acquire spiritual powers. Similarly, the interest of people on earth usually lies within the scope of what they experience. That is why the extent of their understanding is also limited.

Thus, even if someone acquires spiritual powers and the power of Kanjizai while they are alive, they will never understand a field that they have no experience in, because people do not develop an interest in things they have not experienced. Therefore, if you want to develop the power of Kanjizai to the highest level, you need to be aware of the many different worlds that exist. Without this preparation, you will never truly understand everything.

Chapter 5

The Ultimate Form of Kanjizai

1
The Road to God or Buddha

Three types of proof that show whether a person is a messenger of God or Buddha

In this book, I have been discussing Kanjizai, which is an advanced form of spiritual power that comes with attaining enlightenment. Kanjizai, in its ultimate form, allows you to reach the farthest land on the Other Shore, where God or Buddha resides. Thus, we can say that the ultimate power of Kanjizai is the road that leads to God or Buddha.

Since ancient times, humans have been learning various teachings of Buddha's Truth while undergoing numerous reincarnations. During these times, we have also experienced miracles and mysterious phenomena. There have been many miracles in Buddhism and Christianity, and even in more ancient civilizations. Whenever Buddha's Truth was taught, miracles occurred. So the question is, why do miracles occur when Buddha's Truth is being taught? I would like to talk about this now.

As I have already explained in other books, when God sends down His messengers of light to have them preach His teachings, He mainly provides three kinds of proof to show that they are true messengers of God.

The first is *written proof*. This means that the person's writing contains sufficient seeds of knowledge that should be studied as God's Laws. The person must give teachings that can be expressed in writing and recorded for future generations. This is called written proof.

The second is *logical proof*. Just as the term suggests, it means to prove with logic. How so? By proving the Laws that govern the universe created by God. Therefore, logical proof requires a scientific explanation of the world created by God. The Laws must be explained in a way that makes theoretical sense. This is called logical proof.

The third is *actual proof*. Just as the word "actual" suggests, it refers to miracles that can be seen, felt, and heard. By performing miracles, the person gains credibility as a messenger of God.

True Laws, God's Laws, or Buddha's Truth are always accompanied by these three types of proof: written proof, logical proof, and actual proof. However, the weight that is placed on each form of proof varies from messenger to messenger, as each person has their own area of expertise. To take a few examples, it is said that Buddha's spiritual entity focuses on providing written proof; Jesus Christ's spiritual entity is strong at providing logical proof; and Moses' spiritual entity is competent at demonstrating actual proof. Of course, the true teachings contain all three of these kinds of proof, but how much weight is placed on each one depends on who the messenger is.

The power of Kanjizai possessed by Buddha

While it is said that Shakyamuni Buddha had expertise in written proof, he also possessed the power of Kanjizai, which is the topic of this book. What exactly was the power of Kanjizai that he possessed? What kinds of abilities did he have? In this section, I would like to explain Shakyamuni Buddha's power of Kanjizai by breaking it down into several categories.

✦ Mind-reading

The first and most distinct feature of Shakyamuni Buddha's abilities was mind-reading. He is said to have possessed an exceptional ability to read people's minds.

In Shakyamuni's time, many people devoted themselves to him because he made accurate remarks about things. For example, he would guide people by saying things like, "Right now, you have these thoughts, but they are wrong from this perspective. So, you should think like this instead, and things will improve." Or, he would note things like, "Such-and-such must have happened to you when you were a teenager. Someone must have told you so-and-so. Your parents must have raised you in this way." In this way, Shakyamuni Buddha was able to accurately tell various things about people, which is why they believed in him. We can say that his ability to read people's minds was part of his power of Kanjizai.

✦ Past-life-reading

Shakyamuni Buddha was also particularly good at past-life-reading. He often told people he met about their past lives by saying things like, "In your past life, you were born in such-and-such a place and led such-and-such a life. The people here with you now were your friends at that time; you have met them again in this lifetime through the threads of fate." He also told his disciples how they came to join his group through the spiritual ties from their past lives. This power to see into the past is another ability that comes with Kanjizai.

✦ The ability to foresee the future

The Lotus Sutra has descriptions of Shakyamuni Buddha talking about the future. For example, he told some of his famous disciples that they would become tathagatas after several reincarnations—this is called the "Bestowal of Prophecy." It is not clear whether he saw such a vision using his foresight or whether he meant that they simply had the potential to become tathagatas. Regardless, it is clearly recorded in Buddhist scriptures that he was able to see into the future.

✦ Clairvoyance

Another ability of Kanjizai that Shakyamuni Buddha possessed was illustrated by the white light he could emit from between his eyebrows, which is often mentioned in Buddhist scriptures. There is the following story: "A white light shot out from between Shakyamuni's eyebrows. When the light illuminated the world below, it revealed all kinds of underground worlds; when it shone on the world above, it showed heavenly deities. He had the ability to illuminate these worlds." Considering that this story has been handed down, most of his disciples also had spiritual abilities that allowed them to see those worlds.

What was special about Shakyamuni Buddha's clairvoyance was that it enabled him to see the depths of hell and the upper reaches of heaven. We can consider this level of clairvoyance to be part of his power of Kanjizai.

As mentioned above, Shakyamuni Buddha demonstrated his power of Kanjizai in several ways. Although he did not place much importance on spiritual powers in general, he sometimes used these powers to fully explain and show people the worlds beyond this one.

Authenticity as a preacher of the Laws

There are several roads that lead us to God or Buddha, but it is absolutely necessary to use expedient means to educate as many people as possible. The most important thing when using expedient means is the authenticity of the preacher of the Laws. It is essential that they prove their authenticity or, in other words, show that they are a true tathagata, true Buddha, or a person truly sent by God. The power of Kanjizai sometimes serves to prove to people that someone is an authentic preacher of the Laws.

2
An Important Attribute of God

The power to see through and understand everything

In the previous section, I talked about the road to God. Now, I would like to discuss the attributes of God, as doing so will help you understand the power of Kanjizai much better.

We can describe God's attributes in various ways, such as light, love, mercy, kindness, courage, beauty, goodness, and hope. But I believe there is an important attribute that we must not overlook, which is the power to see through everything. Put simply, it is the power to know all things or the power of omniscience.

God illuminates the whole world, but this does not just mean that He is shining light onto it. To illuminate something means to shine light on something. When something receives light, it becomes visible, and when it is visible, it can be identified. Simply put, the idea that God is universal light, or that He is the light that shines on all things, suggests that God can see everything as a result of shining His light. This ability to see through everything and identify every detail is also an attribute of God.

The difference between people of high spiritual levels and people of low spiritual levels

Now, let us shift our attention to people living in the earthly world. What kinds of people appear to be of a high spiritual level and a low spiritual level? I would like to contemplate this point.

First, let us think about people who are of a low spiritual level. In most cases, they think in an animalistic way. What do I mean by that? I mean that they only think about how to protect themselves, how to fulfill their selfish desires, or how to benefit themselves. This way of thinking has been considered extremely shameful in religion since ancient times. Some people are only concerned about themselves and their own benefit, or are only interested in things that please their eyes and tongue and satisfy their desires. They are considered people of low spiritual levels.

In a nutshell, people of low spiritual levels cannot see themselves, others, or the world in the right way. They have very little ability to understand things. Their ability is so limited that they cannot even understand themselves. In other words, their light is too weak to illuminate the world, or even to shed light on themselves.

Then, what are the attributes of people of high spiritual levels? They can see, hear, and understand a wide range of things; they can express their opinions based on their rich experiences, abundant knowledge, and high levels of awareness. What is more, their opinions not only serve to benefit themselves but can also raise the level of humanity as a whole. This means they possess the ability to see through and identify things by shedding light on them, which is similar to God's attribute.

Among the various attributes of God, the ability to see through and identify everything is an extremely important ability. We must never forget it. This ability can also be expressed as "awareness" in ordinary terms. It can be described as the ability to perceive, understand, feel, and digest various things. In the end, we can say that the source of Kanjizai is found in this very attribute of God. Kanjizai ultimately leads to God's ability to illuminate and identify all things, that is, to find out everything by shedding light onto it all.

3
Love and Mercy

The similarities and differences between love and mercy

Since I have discussed God's attributes, let me now talk about love and mercy. Love and mercy are also major attributes of God that have been considered important in Christianity and Buddhism. In this section, I would like to focus on the relationship between Kanjizai and love and mercy, and how Kanjizai affects or is affected by these attributes.

Before delving into the topic, let me start by talking about the similarities and differences between love and mercy. Love and mercy are often used interchangeably because they are both forces that work to benefit others. They are indeed powers that make other people better, more wonderful, more joyful, and happier. If I were to point out the differences, I would say that love is more of a power that draws people together, nurtures them, and unites them to work hand in hand, while mercy is more of a vertical light that comes from above, or a great power that flows from up high to down low. You could also say that mercy is light that is given to humans by God.

As I explain in the Theory of the Developmental Stages of Love in my other books, love has different stages. There are four of them: love that gives, which is fundamental love; nurturing love; forgiving love; and love incarnate. I teach that you should start by giving love to others, gradually develop yourself to practice the love of a leader, grow spiritually to be able to exert the love of a religious leader, and finally, attain the level of love incarnate to become the ethos or spirit of the age. When humans reach the level of love incarnate, their love turns into mercy. Thus, I expound the Theory of the Developmental Stages of Love as an idea that combines the horizontal power of love and the vertical power of mercy.

The relationship between Kanjizai and the developmental stages of love

Next, how is Kanjizai related to the developmental structure of the two major concepts of love and mercy? How does the power of Kanjizai differ from the developmental stages of love? Do they share any similarities? In the developmental stages of love, I refer to fundamental love as love of the fifth dimension. Below that is instinctive love, which is love of the fourth dimension. I also explain that nurturing love belongs to the sixth dimension, forgiving love to the seventh dimension, and love incarnate to the eighth dimension. There is also love of the ninth dimension, which is called love of the Savior. How, then, is the power of Kanjizai related to each of these stages of love? Let us consider this.

As you may expect, there is a certain degree of correlation between the power of Kanjizai and the development of love. The development of love can also be described as the development of one's character. As you develop and elevate your character and become closer to God or Buddha, you will also enhance your power of Kanjizai. This is the true nature of Kanjizai. So, if you are on the right track, your power of Kanjizai will be enhanced as you raise the level of your love. The more love you have, the more power of Kanjizai you will gain as a "tool" to realize and practice love.

The power of Rojin will elevate Kanjizai into true love

That being said, I must also point out the opposite aspect of Kanjizai, which is that your love dies when your power of Kanjizai degrades to a mere psychic power or becomes a subject of blind faith. This can happen because Kanjizai has a tremendous power to attract people's attention and enchant them, but it can be a double-edged sword. A sword can be used as either a "life-taking sword" or a "life-giving sword," which also applies to Kanjizai. If used well, Kanjizai can bring benefits to others, but if used wrongly, it can kill or hurt them. Kanjizai is incredibly powerful, indeed.

The dangerous side of Kanjizai is obvious when we review the past evildoings of religious groups in the world. If you carefully observe newly established religious groups, you will see that their believers lose their minds after becoming obsessed with psychic powers. Because Kanjizai is a power that transcends time and space, many who wield it can lose a sense of reality and become ungrounded. This is expected. Just imagine how difficult it would be to lead a sound daily life when you can see spirits that are invisible to the physical eyes, hear their voices, and perceive the Spirit World. It would be a very difficult life to live. That is why it is necessary to put the "sword" of Kanjizai into its "sheath." Doing so corresponds to the practice of Rojin.

Both Kanjizai and Rojin have tremendous power as "swords," but Kanjizai is like an unsheathed sword, while Rojin is like a sheathed sword. So, when your power of Kanjizai grows in proportion to the level of your love, you must eventually learn to turn your power of Kanjizai into the power of Rojin. This means that, to elevate your power of Kanjizai into true love, you need to use your will to control your power of Kanjizai and adjust it as necessary. To do this, you must first master the power of Rojin. Only when you have mastered Rojin can you develop your power of Kanjizai to the height of mercy. In other words, by mastering Rojin, you can turn your God-like spiritual power into mercy that can truly save others. So, while Kanjizai developed in the wrong direction will lead you to a life of self-protection and self-appraisal, true Kanjizai forged through the stage of Rojin will develop or ascend into mercy.

4
The Centripetal Force of the Universe

So far, I have talked about the power of Kanjizai from various angles within the ambit of the universe. To tell you the truth, there are two main forces at work in the universe—*centripetal* force and *centrifugal* force.

Centripetal force is the power that binds independently acting bodies to create harmony and order. It works to unite things that would otherwise scatter apart and become useless, and maintain a harmonious and orderly state. This force manifests in various teachings. For example, in the teaching of love, it manifests as a method to harmonize relationships with others; in the teaching of order and propriety, it manifests as a way to maintain orderly relationships. These teachings are the manifestations of the centripetal force of the universe. In fact, the teachings left by many people throughout history were about this force. To figure out how to harmonize, unite, and bring order to the universe has been the core theme of Buddha's Truth.

To further study this force, we must think about its hidden purpose. What is the purpose of the centripetal force of the universe? When we explore this, we come to understand that it is securing a place for our soul training. In the universe, various planets exist in a balanced state, and humans, animals, and plants can survive on them in harmony. This very fact shows that centripetal force is securing and providing a place for us to train our souls. It is creating an environment that allows many souls to continuously undergo spiritual training, and by doing so, it provides an opportunity for love to be reproduced in abundance. It creates a space in which love can be reproduced in many ways.

Thus, centripetal force mainly works to create the natural environment and the social environment. The real purpose of this force of the universe is to create these types of environments.

On the other hand, what is centrifugal force? I would like to talk about this in the next section.

5
The Centrifugal Force of the Universe

The purpose and the two aspects of centrifugal force

I explained that the centripetal force of the universe corresponds to the act of love and the act of harmony. What, then, is the centrifugal force of the universe? Considering centripetal force is the power that tries to bind scattering entities together to establish harmony and order, we can naturally deduce that centrifugal force is the power that tries to disperse things and carry them even further away. Then, why does this force exist in the universe? What kinds of power does it have? I would like to think about this point.

Let me first talk about its purpose. Centrifugal force exists to bring about progress and evolution. Although connecting entities and bringing order to them certainly creates a wonderful environment, simply creating and maintaining it can lead to inertia and preserve the status quo. Although people may be able to live in joy and happiness in an environment like this, those feelings will eventually fade, and people will grow bored. That is why there is a need for change in the environment. To bring about change, elements such as progress, development, and evolution are needed.

In this way, the universe is full of contradictory forces; at times, things try to contract, while at other times, they try to expand and disperse. These two contradictory forces exist everywhere in this great universe.

In what kind of teaching does this centrifugal force manifest? How does this prevailing force in the universe work? I believe there are two essential aspects to this force. The first is the fact that every human being has their own unique character. This enables people to compete with each other and refine themselves for their soul training. We could call this the "principle of friendly competition." This principle works to promote the evolution of the universe. As people compete with each other, they strive to advance, even one or two steps further. Competition through friendly rivalry is given to humans as a law or principle of evolution and progress.

The other aspect of centrifugal force, seen from a completely different perspective, can be expressed using the word "prosperity." While harmony and order look well-kept and wonderful, they are a long way from creating powerful happiness. Achieving or creating powerful happiness means creating a prosperous society. It also means making wonderful things shine brilliantly in various ways. As we progress, evolve, and develop, we prosper as a result. I believe the principle of the universe can only become complete when it incorporates this idea of prosperity.

Kanjizai—centrifugal force,
Rojin—centripetal force

I have discussed the centripetal and centrifugal forces that prevail in the universe. How, then, is the power of Kanjizai related to these two major forces? Have you ever thought about this?

When considering the two vectors that are working in the universe, Kanjizai corresponds to the outward-facing vector, namely, the centrifugal force. It is the power that works to develop the universe and make it more prosperous. It is the power that boosts human abilities, broadens their views of the world, and expands their field of spiritual activity. In contrast, when you use your spiritual power in the direction of realizing love and harmony, it becomes Rojin, the other type of advanced spiritual power.

In conclusion, we can say that, although both Kanjizai and Rojin contain advanced spiritual powers at their core, they work in different directions. Kanjizai is directed outward, which leads to the evolution, development, and prosperity of the universe, while Rojin is directed inward to realize love, harmony, and order. It is important that these two powers are kept in balance and that they work to help other people, and at the same time, serve as encouragement and tools for the people who live as fighters of God.

Chapter 6

The State of God-as-Self

1
Kanjizai and Nyoshin

The state of Kanjizai is like having two eyes, whereas the state of Nyoshin is like having multiple eyes

In this chapter, I would like to talk about the state that leads to the enlightenment of *God-as-self*, which I touched upon in Chapter One. As a prerequisite to understanding this, let me first explain Kanjizai and Nyoshin.

As I already mentioned, you start to possess the power of Kanjizai when you attain the enlightenment of the Brahma Realm, which can also be called the enlightenment of Kanjizai. But, of course, the basic power of Kanjizai can be attained in the state of arhat. I also mentioned a state called Nyoshin. While Nyoshin is mainly the state of tathagata, it is also possible for a bodhisattva to partially hold this state. Now, what exactly is the difference between Kanjizai and Nyoshin? I would like to talk about this in terms of the enlightenment and spiritual abilities associated with these states.

The major difference between the enlightenment of Kanjizai and that of Nyoshin is the breadth of interest. The main point of Kanjizai is how the person senses things with that power. It is still at this level. But the state of Nyoshin is

《The Relationship between Kanjizai and Nyoshin》

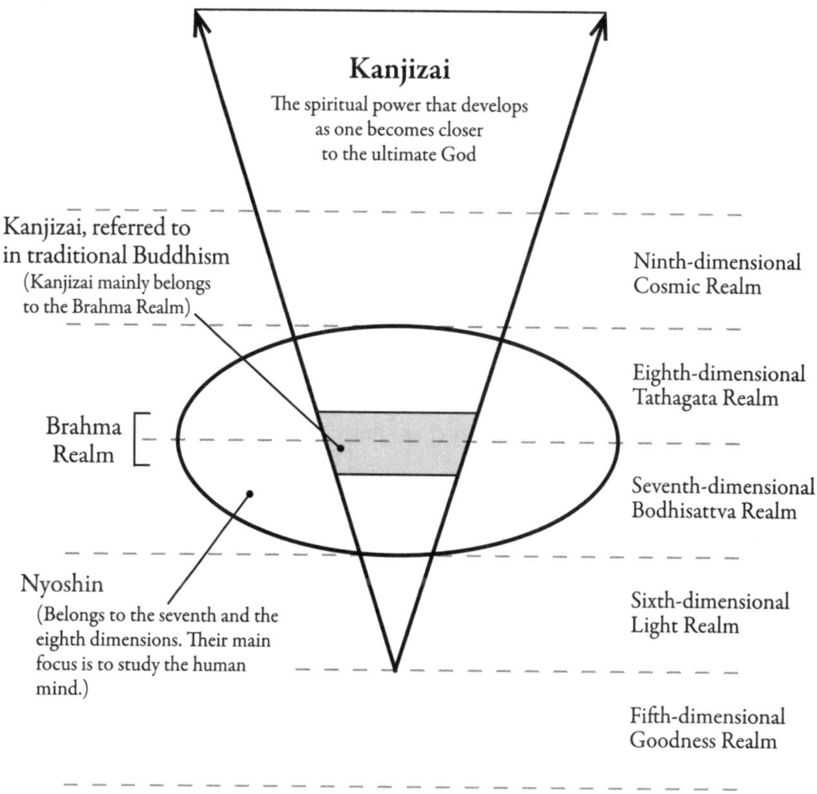

- Spirits in the sixth dimension can begin to possess Kanjizai, and the power develops increasingly as they proceed to higher dimensions. But sometimes, Kanjizai only refers to the spiritual power possessed by those in the Brahma Realm.

- The power of Nyoshin spans from the seventh-dimensional Bodhisattva Realm to the eighth-dimensional Tathagata Realm.

▲This chart is based on the illustration the author drew when he was explaining Kanjizai and Nyoshin during the "Thursday Seminar" in November 1988. The seminar was on Chapter Four of *The Laws of the Sun*.

a little different from that. Those with the enlightenment of Kanjizai use their power while retaining their physical senses or tactile sensations; they perceive things using their two eyes, two ears, and two hands. In contrast, those in the state of Nyoshin acquire senses that are different from physical senses. Figuratively speaking, the state of Nyoshin is like having multiple eyes; it feels as if you have many eyes dispatched in different places. On the other hand, the state of Kanjizai is like having two eyes on tentacles, similar to snails; they freely extend to places and allow you to look around. But when you are in the state of Nyoshin, it feels as if your eyes are being teleported to various places, allowing you to see and perceive things in those places on the spot.

Looking at others from your point of view or from theirs

In the state of Nyoshin, you can say that your spiritual powers are no longer restricted by the physical senses.

In the state of Kanjizai, your consciousness is still bound to your physical senses, so you can freely perceive things but only within the framework of your physical senses. On the other hand, when you reach the state of Nyoshin, you no longer rely on such senses. You will know things as if your mind has dispersed or teleported freely and appeared in various places. Thus, people who have reached the state of Nyoshin can perceive things in a more multidimensional and realistic way.

Those with Kanjizai and Nyoshin also understand other people's feelings in different ways. When you have reached Kanjizai, you look at others from your point of view and understand extensively the thoughts and feelings of others, or their past, present, and future. But in the case of Nyoshin, you put yourself in other people's shoes. When you have attained Nyoshin, you can intentionally diversify your consciousness, split it into many pieces, and send those pieces to different places.

There is not so much difference between Kanjizai and Nyoshin in terms of *what* you understand about others. But in fact, there is a tremendous difference in terms of *how deeply* you understand others when you put yourself in their viewpoint, as opposed to when you look at them from your own.

Therefore, when you have attained the enlightenment of Nyoshin, you can exert the power of Kanjizai while completely transcending your physical senses. This is what I mean when I say, "Nyoshin represents the enlightenment of tathagata." To attain the enlightenment of tathagata means to be in tune with the consciousness of God, while also being a completely free spiritual entity. In other words, tathagatas do not need to use their physical senses to perceive things. They have the ability to freely expand their awareness as consciousnesses, spirits, and souls. On the other hand, the souls in the Bodhisattva Realm still retain some degree of their physical senses. This is where the two differ.

So, we can say that Nyoshin is the manifestation of the enlightenment of *one is many, many are one.* It is the state in which you can multiply your consciousness into many entities and have them exist everywhere. It is like creating many copies of yourself. When someone with Nyoshin tries to understand others, they multiply their consciousness and have them freely move to multiple places. This is the difference in the degree of understanding between Kanjizai and Nyoshin. It may be very difficult to comprehend this logically, but I hope you can sense what I mean.

2
Nyoshin and the State of Universe-as-Self

Transporting the core part of the consciousness versus expanding the consciousness itself

I just mentioned that Nyoshin refers to the state of enlightenment and the spiritual abilities of tathagatas. Now, let us compare these with the enlightenment of *universe-as-self* and the spiritual ability that comes with it.

It is said that Gautama Siddhartha, otherwise known as Shakyamuni Buddha, experienced becoming one with the universe when he attained Great Enlightenment in India nearly 2,600 years ago. At that time, it had been six years since he had renounced the world. One night, he had been meditating deeply under a big Pipal tree until dawn, when he suddenly felt his consciousness expanding. He felt it outgrow his body and become larger and larger, as if he were becoming a giant. Before long, his spiritual body grew to a few hundred feet in size to the point where he was looking down at his physical body sitting under the Pipal tree. Even more amazingly, his spiritual body continued to grow until he was overlooking the flowing Ganges River and the various towns in the distance. His spiritual body continued to expand until it was larger than the Earth, at which point he was looking down upon the Earth from far above. This is the enlightenment of universe-as-self that Shakyamuni experienced.

So, what is the difference between this stage of enlightenment and the stage of Nyoshin? Some of you may have already noticed the difference. I explained that tathagatas have the spiritual ability to disperse and concentrate their consciousness at will, as expressed by the phrase, "one is many, many are one." This is where the difference lies: someone at the stage of Nyoshin is able to freely disperse and concentrate their consciousness, whereas someone at the stage of universe-as-self is able to expand their consciousness to the size of the universe.

At the level of Nyoshin, you can disperse and concentrate yourself as a spiritual entity, which means you can transport the core part of your consciousness anywhere, like a moving dot. On the other hand, at the level of universe-as-self, the core part of your consciousness, or your consciousness itself, enlarges and expands. This is a much higher level of enlightenment and spiritual ability. To put it differently, when you are in the state of universe-as-self, your consciousness grows large enough to encompass the entire Earth. This is not something that ordinary people can experience; it is a truly significant religious experience that allows you to feel as if you have become God or Buddha.

The state of universe-as-self is the enlightenment of a savior

Historically speaking, not many people have experienced the state of universe-as-self. I just gave the example of Shakyamuni Buddha, but in truth, it was not just him who had experienced it; several others have also undergone it. One of them was Jesus Christ, though he did not mention it in his sermons. The Bible has no description of his experience of universe-as-self, but in truth, he experienced it at the age of 30 before leaving Qumran to preach the Law. While he was meditating in a cave, he experienced his consciousness looking down on his body from a great height before reaching and entering the heavenly world. This was not a mere out-of-body experience; he experienced the state of an archangel or God. Because of this experience, he was able to deepen his awareness of himself as a savior.

Another historical figure was Confucius of China, but his case was different. His version of universe-as-self was not about space but about his consciousness within. As Confucius studied academically, elevated his enlightenment, and raised his intellectual level, he felt his insight developing extensively. He was able to understand many things clearly and even reached a state where he could understand the consciousness of *Tiandi* (the Emperor of Heaven), the Creator God. At this level of awareness, he was able to grasp the fate of humankind living on Earth and their way of life extremely well. He could understand these things as if he were looking at ants in the palm of his hand.

Moses, who received the Ten Commandments from Yahweh on Mount Sinai, also experienced a kind of universe-as-self. He had been meditating for dozens of days when he experienced his consciousness leaving his physical body; it grew enormously, surpassing Mount Sinai, until he was looking down on the Earth from above. Through this experience, Moses also became aware even more clearly that he was a savior.

Zoroaster, also known as Zarathustra, who was born in the Middle East, had exactly the same experience. Zarathustra taught fire worship, which was the teachings of fire. The reason he taught such teachings was because he experienced, himself, becoming an enormous fire when he attained enlightenment. One night, as he went deeper into meditation, he felt his spiritual body turning into a gigantic light like a rising flame. It continued to rise up to 150 feet, then to 300 feet, and eventually turned into a gigantic pillar of fire. His spiritual body had turned into a pillar of fire that rose up to ten thousand feet or higher. After this, he gained mystical, spiritual powers and learned many truths. I intend to publish books about him in more detail in the future. He was also one of those people who experienced universe-as-self in a different way.

In addition to the people I mentioned, lots of others experienced universe-as-self in ancient civilizations, although their names have not been handed down to the present day. In any case, I can assure you that this state of universe-as-self is the enlightenment of a savior.

3
Different Stages of Universe-as-Self

In the previous section, I mentioned that the awareness of universe-as-self is the enlightenment of a savior. But when you look at this state in more detail, you see that there are different stages to the enlightenment of universe-as-self. In this section, I will explain them, starting from the first stage.

The first stage: Looking down on the Earth from far above

To tell the truth, the first stage of universe-as-self can also be experienced by beings of the Sun Realm, that is, people in the highest level of the eighth-dimensional Tathagata Realm. What they experience is not merely an out-of-body experience but a much higher state. They will find themselves looking down on the earthly world from high above. We can call this the first stage of universe-as-self.

In history, Socrates of ancient Greece experienced this stage. He supposedly experienced looking down on the Earth. He would sometimes enter a meditative state while walking outside and stand there motionless for a day or two. He even stood motionless on the battlefield in a war. During these times, his soul left his physical body and traveled freely in the sky, far above. So, not only did he undergo an out-of-body experience, but he also had an experience of looking down on the Earth from far above. He was an inhabitant of the Sun Realm, so, in this way, we can say that even the inhabitants of the Sun Realm are able to experience universe-as-self. This is the first stage.

The second stage: The state of galaxy-as-self

Then, what is the second stage of universe-as-self? In this stage, you are not just looking down on the Earth, but your spiritual consciousness expands to the size of the galaxy. In other words, your awareness expands to the galactic level. At this level, you not only look down on the Earth but also perceive it as a tiny cell of your own body. This is the second stage of universe-as-self. It is the enlightenment of the lower level of the ninth dimension.

It is said that there are ten spirits in the ninth dimension. In principle, they can be classified as "higher-level spirits" and "lower-level spirits," but the distinction is not simply the difference in their spiritual level. Rather, it represents the difference in the work they did in this earthly world.

Shakyamuni Buddha resides in the upper level of front heaven in the ninth dimension. His core consciousness is called El Cantare (Grand Tathagata Shakyamuni), who is connected to the worlds above the ninth dimension, all the way up to the Primordial Buddha. El Cantare is the one who created the structure and laws of the universe. He has been guiding the planet Earth as the Supreme God since the creation of the Earth Spirit Group, and He invited the other nine ninth-dimensional spirits to the Earth.

The spirits of Jesus Christ (Amor) and Confucius (Therabim) also reside in the upper realm of the front side of the ninth dimension. They both bear responsibility for the current civilization on Earth and often give direct guidance. This is because they have outstanding achievements and are at a very high spiritual level.

Besides these, there are spirits that currently reside in the lower level of the ninth dimension, but this does not necessarily mean that their spiritual level is lower compared to other ninth-dimensional spirits. Rather, it means they play a secondary or an assisting role in this particular civilization. Historically, there have been many times when the members of the upper and lower realms of the ninth dimension have switched around. The spirits who are now residing in the lower realm are Manu, Maitreya, Newton, Zeus, and Zoroaster. Their enlightenment corresponds to the second stage of universe-as-self, which is also called *galaxy-as-self*. They have attained a level of enlightenment that allows them to expand their awareness to the galactic level.

Other than those mentioned above, the spirits of Moses (Moria) and Enlil reside in the rear side of the heavenly world.

(Author's Note: To further explain the spirits of the ninth dimension, their difference is not about their spiritual level but the role they play in each civilization. Currently, Jesus and his line of angels are strongly supporting El Cantare, but the rest are not active as much. The branch spirits of El Cantare reside in the higher realm of the ninth dimension as personified gods. At this point in time, particular spirits like Gaia are able to go back and forth between the eighth and ninth dimensions to serve as assistants of El Cantare. Depending on the civilization, these spirits may take on a more leading role than Zoroaster, Manu, Maitreya, and Zeus. Currently, the powers of Moses and Confucius are slightly weakened, and as for Enlil, his power is sealed for now.)

The third stage: Your consciousness expands to the ends of the universe

What, then, is the third stage of universe-as-self[1]? It is the mysterious experience that Shakyamuni Buddha underwent during his time in India. Not only did his consciousness expand to be large enough for him to look down on the Earth and grow to the size of the galaxy, but it also kept expanding to the point where he was able to see the ends of the universe. His consciousness expanded until he was able to perceive the size of the entire universe.

People who undergo this spiritual experience will know that our galaxy serves as God's heart. The galaxy is like the heart organ of God, and each star or planet is just one of the cells that make up the heart.

Historically, very few people have achieved this third stage of universe-as-self while they were alive. Some had the potential to experience it but did not. To tell the truth, only one spirit in the higher level of the ninth dimension experienced this state during their life in this world—Shakyamuni Buddha. No one else has experienced it while living with a physical body.

This is the explanation of the different stages of the enlightenment of universe-as-self.

[Editor's note]

1 Chapter One explained that the enlightenment of universe-as-self comes in two stages. Chapter Six provides further explanation by dividing the second stage into two parts.

4
The State of God-as-Self

Perceiving yourself as the laws of the universe

Now, I would like to talk about the next stage. I do not think there are any documents that describe this state, nor has anyone experienced it. The state of enlightenment that lies above the state of universe-as-self is the state of *God-as-self.* This is the enlightenment of the tenth dimension. Although a ninth-dimensional spirit may partially experience this state of God-as-self, it is difficult to experience it fully. But if the spirit has the potential to ascend to the tenth dimension, it should know what the state of God-as-self is.

The enlightenment of the tenth dimension is no longer a human-level enlightenment. It is a state in which you can perceive yourself as part of the laws of the universe. In this state, not only do you perceive the third-dimensional, spatial expanse of the universe and become aware of your spiritual consciousness expanding to the size of the universe, but you also recognize yourself as part of the laws flowing and governing the universe.

Having said this, the Laws of the Primordial Buddha (Primordial God) are a tremendous number of bundles of light and a collection of an enormous number of principles, so there is no single consciousness that can ever fully understand and encompass them all. But when you become aware that you are playing a part or a role in the workings of the universe, in other words, that you are part of these enormous laws of the Primordial Buddha that govern the universe, you have achieved the state of God-as-self.

The role of the tenth-dimensional consciousnesses of the Earth

Let us take the Earth, for example. There are three consciousnesses in the Earth's tenth-dimensional world: the Grand Sun Consciousness, the Moon Consciousness, and the Earth Consciousness. Indeed, they are all spirits of planetary consciousness, but they are not simply material or physical consciousnesses, or souls or spirits that govern the planet. They are also each in charge of one aspect of the laws of the universe.

✦ The Grand Sun Consciousness promotes positivity

The Grand Sun Consciousness plays the role of a positive consciousness or the consciousness of *yang*. This spirit has awakened to its mission of embodying the positive aspect of the Laws of the Primordial Buddha. It has a role in promoting positivity everywhere it influences.

✦ The Moon Consciousness adds depth

The Moon Consciousness is said to govern grace and femininity, and it is also the source of art. These elements are governed by the Moon Consciousness. In contrast to the *yang* side represented by the Grand Sun Consciousness, the Moon Consciousness can be said to represent the *yin* side. Stated differently, it has the role of adding depth to things.

In the end, what does the Moon Consciousness signify? We can say that it represents harmony. The Moon Consciousness embodies a part of the Laws that create harmony in the great universe.

✦ The Earth Consciousness reproduces and nurtures

Last but not least, what is the role of the Earth Consciousness? It plays a role in providing a learning place for various life forms. Within the Laws of the Primordial Buddha, it is in charge of prosperity. The Earth Consciousness has the role of reproducing and nurturing various living beings.

The state of God-as-self for the Earth's tenth-dimensional consciousnesses

Let me summarize what I have explained so far. The Grand Sun Consciousness embodies the principles of progress and evolution within the Laws of the Primordial Buddha. These two principles run throughout the universe. The Grand Sun Consciousness can intuitively perceive the principles of progress and evolution that govern not only the Earth but also the entire universe. This is the enlightenment of the Grand Sun Consciousness and the state of God-as-self that it experiences.

The enlightenment of God-as-self for the Moon Consciousness is the ability to perceive all of the consciousnesses of harmony that govern the universe. The Moon Consciousness can expand its consciousness to the size of the universe and grasp all harmony and order that flows through the entire universe.

What, then, is the enlightenment of God-as-self for the Earth Consciousness? There are many planets in this vast universe that provide an environment to nurture life. The enlightenment of the Earth Consciousness is to recognize the creation of the environment and the realization of prosperity on each planet. It does not simply recognize prosperity on the planet Earth but can also perceive the principle of prosperity that runs through the entire universe. This is the state of God-as-self for the Earth Consciousness in the tenth dimension.

From what I have explained so far, you can probably see that there are still some limitations even in the state of God-as-self. So the next question is, what happens if these limitations are removed?

5
The True Identity of God

How Buddhism and Christianity recognize God or Buddha

In the previous section, I explained three different states of God-as-self at the level of the Grand Sun Consciousness, the Moon Consciousness, and the Earth Consciousness. Out of the three, the Grand Sun Consciousness is at the highest spiritual level. Therefore, we can say that, out of the three consciousnesses, the Grand Sun Consciousness has attained the highest level of enlightenment of God-as-self. Moreover, in the Spirit Group of this Solar System, there exists a "parent" that gave birth to this Grand Sun Consciousness—the Solar System Consciousness of the eleventh dimension. It is the spiritual consciousness of the Sun we see in the sky.

Now, the questions are: What is God or Buddha that we humans refer to? What defines God or Buddha? What did Jesus Christ mean by God? What kind of existence is the Primordial Buddha that Buddhism mentions? Let us think about these points.

I am almost certain that the Grand Sun Consciousness of the tenth dimension is the real identity of "God" or "Buddha" that the past religions in this earthly world have referred to. It is most certainly true that the "God without human characteristics" that religions mention is the Grand Sun Consciousness.

In Buddhism, there is faith in Mahavairocana Buddha, who is considered the Primordial Buddha of the great universe. In reality, Mahavairocana Buddha is none other than the Grand Sun Consciousness of the tenth dimension. It means that Buddhism recognized the existence of this tenth-dimensional consciousness.

On the contrary, the Christian concept of God is a little different. Here lies the major difference between Buddhism and Christianity. Because Jesus only had a short time to deepen his enlightenment, we can assume that his understanding of God was limited to the ninth-dimensional level. The Supreme God El Cantare is a being connected to the worlds above the ninth dimension, but when Jesus lived in a physical body, he referred to El Cantare as "My Father" or "My Abba." But of course, he seemed to have felt intuitively, or rather, he was fairly confident that there was an even greater being than the God he was speaking to. The consciousness that he called "Father" had human characteristics and was a spiritual being with emotions. So, Jesus sensed that the Creator of the universe must be an even greater consciousness. However, it seems that during his lifetime, Jesus could not reach the level of enlightenment needed to recognize that greater Being. This is the reason why Christianity is said to be a monotheistic religion with faith in a personified God. In any case, how God is recognized depends on the level of enlightenment that the awakened ones have reached.

Where does the true Creator or the God of Origin reside?

When we try to unveil the true identity of God in a theoretical book like this, unfortunately, we cannot say that the consciousness of the tenth dimension or even the eleventh-dimensional consciousness of our Solar System is God Himself. After all, they are "consciousnesses" and not God. This means they are also spiritual beings that have split off from God.

Then, what about the Galactic Consciousness of the twelfth dimension? Indeed, this consciousness is even more evolved than the Solar System Consciousness, but we cannot say that it is God, either. What about the thirteenth-dimensional Cosmic Spirit? This being is extremely close to God, so from the perspective of humans living on Earth, it can be referred to as God. However, the truth is that this space of the thirteenth-dimensional universe has a limited size like a container, and the thirteenth-dimensional being only governs this particular space. This shows that there is a limit even to this being. In other words, what humans recognize as the great universe itself is nothing more than the physical body of this thirteenth-dimensional being.

Therefore, even the thirteenth-dimensional existence is considered "God with limitations" and cannot be called "God that has no beginning or end." What is more, as far as I know, there are multiple cosmic spirits referred to as thirteenth-dimensional consciousnesses. From a higher perspective, the great universe that contains the Earth and our galaxy appears like a football or a fish tank. Our universe is like an isolated world that is floating within a much larger world. That is the reality. So you must know that there are multiple consciousnesses in the thirteenth dimension.

Then, you may wonder whether the fourteenth-dimensional consciousness is the true God. Truthfully speaking, the fourteenth-dimensional consciousness encompasses and governs numerous thirteenth-dimensional football-like universes. So, even the fourteenth-dimensional consciousness merely makes up a universe that is one level higher.

As you explore God more in this way, you may speculate where the real Creator resides. From what I can perceive, the

God (Buddha) of Origin is a Being of at least the twentieth dimension or higher. According to what I have heard from the higher spirits, which is based on what they heard in legends, the universe does not end at just the twentieth or thirtieth dimension but has a dimensional structure that extends to much higher worlds. So, unfortunately, we do not know the truth beyond that level. All I can say is that the higher the dimension, the greater the awareness of the consciousness becomes, and the larger the space it occupies. In other words, there exists a greater consciousness that far surpasses human understanding.

Therefore, all I can say at this point in time is that humans are small, dot-like creatures with unique characters, who are being nurtured within the magnificent and transcendent consciousness. This is as far as we can go in understanding the true identity of God or the Primordial Buddha.

Chapter 7

A Lecture on *Kanjizai*

Lecture given on February 26, 1989
at Hotel Kizankan, Tokyo

1
The Intention behind the Publication of *Kanjizai*

Kanjizai *reveals the Truth that transcends personal experience and enlightenment*

I believe that the most unique feature of Happy Science is the systematized Laws presented in a way that has never been seen before. Rather than adhering to and promoting a single teaching as the absolute principle, what we intend to do is reorganize the various teachings of the Truth that exist in the Real World, as well as ideas taught in the earthly world that are based on those true teachings. Moreover, we hope to leave those teachings and ideas as a legacy not only for the people of today but also for the people of future generations.

As you study these systematized Laws, you will probably find some of them useful to you now and some not. Perhaps you may find some teachings particularly helpful at the time you study them. Regardless, I would like you to avidly study them all because the current age is a precious age in which you can learn various teachings.

The range, profundity, and level of the Laws taught at Happy Science surpass what people can think of, believe, or experience. The enlightenment of some of our teachings is impossible to attain through one's own experiences in this world. However, at this time, Truth that transcends personal wisdom is being revealed directly from the heavenly world.

It is important to learn the Truth humbly and selflessly, especially the parts that cannot be attained through human effort. I do not think there is anyone who can claim to have experienced and learned the entire content of my teachings written in the 2,600 or more books I have published so far (3,250 books have been published as of 2025). I believe a large part of it goes beyond the scope of your personal experience. It is important that you pay respect to this Truth, and learn it with a humble and pure heart. What is more, I hope that you will accurately convey what you have learned and understood to those who come later.

For this reason, people who have studied various kinds of religious teachings, or who are confident in their spiritual knowledge, may not always be evaluated well here in Happy Science. These people need to understand that they are being asked to meet much higher expectations instead of focusing on their own desires. We are not carrying out activities to provide people with a place to simply express their opinions or to realize their personal desires. Rather, our activities are a sacred movement. In fact, it is not just a movement, but a great movement. I am determined to launch a large-scale spiritual movement, and I would also like everyone to be as strongly determined as I am.

Therefore, the work of the lecturers on the Laws from now on is to deeply understand the Truth that is being taught and turn it into "living knowledge." Knowledge remains dormant if it is just left as a writing. What is important is to think about how to awaken it, how to breathe life into it, and how to explain it, talk about it, and convey it to others as Words of Light.

Please know that there is a Truth that transcends personal experience and enlightenment. In fact, I wrote this book *Kanjizai* to allow people to learn it.

Kanjizai *outlines the potential of spiritual powers*

This book was by no means published to boast about the spiritual powers that I possess. I simply outlined what real spiritual power is like and the extent of its potential. I did this because there are too many people in the world who have become absorbed in spiritual matters and overly proud of their psychic power. If we were to compare the power of a so-called psychic and someone with Kanjizai to a sword, the sword of the psychic would most likely chip the moment it touches the great "sword" of Kanjizai. In reality, there is such a significant difference in their powers. I, myself, have no intention of wielding my "mighty sword," but I would like people to know the stark difference between the two.

With this as an introduction, I will move on to the details of Kanjizai.

2
Kanjizai and Love

High spirits sometimes demonstrate the power of Kanjizai to persuade the spirits in hell

The power of Kanjizai is extremely closely connected to our essence as human beings. The power of Kanjizai is indispensable for humans to realize that God resides within us. People living in this world tend to start believing in the world of spirits, God, or Buddha when something deemed impossible happens before their eyes. They often realize that God or Buddha exists by witnessing so-called psychic powers or spiritual phenomena.

On the other hand, Happy Science is trying to convey to people the existence of the Real World, God, and Buddha through the content of our teachings alone, which may rather seem to be an inefficient approach. It may be quicker to convince people by showing them spiritual phenomena. However, we are taking this approach because we believe that it will allow our activities to continue far into the future.

Then, what about in the Real World? For example, do the inhabitants of the fourth dimension really believe in God?

How do they understand the meaning of their world and the worlds that exist above theirs? Truth be told, they still do not understand these things completely because they are not perfect beings, either. That is why, when high spirits come down to the fourth dimension to teach those spirits about God, they sometimes do so by demonstrating various kinds of powers because they think that explaining with just words is not enough to convince them of the Truth.

Let me give you an example from my own experience. When I spoke to the spirits of hell, I found that many of them could not accept that they had actually died, readily admit their mistakes in life, or even acknowledge that they are spirits. That is why I try to guide them by pointing out something that only they would know about or mentioning something I would never know. For example, I tell them, "You died at such-and-such a place about 450 years ago. You had such-and-such a job and lived in such-and-such a place." As I continue to talk about the events and stories of their lives, one after another, they gradually become lost for words and become receptive. At that time, they naturally wonder why I know these things. To wonder why is the key point here. They realize that there are mystical powers beyond their own, and this allows them to gain a new perspective. Even this simple realization can help them stand at the gateway of religious awakening.

However, some people cannot guide the spirits of hell no matter how hard they try to persuade them. If a person's enlightenment is shallow, they will not be able to guide the spirits of hell, even if they are psychic. No matter how much they talk, they cannot convince the spirits. This is because they are not able to fully understand what the spirits went through in the past, what kind of situation these spirits are in, or what types of spirits they are. Unless they know these things, they cannot persuade the spirits and send them to heaven.

Even animal spirits will open up to you if you can understand them

What I just mentioned not only applies to human spirits but also to animal spirits, such as the spirits of snakes and foxes. It is probably very difficult for you to guide these spirits with your current abilities. Guiding animal spirits is indeed more challenging than guiding human spirits. It is incredibly difficult to explain what you have learned in a way that animals can understand because you need to persuade them using limited words and explanations. There are many things animals do not understand. That is why I sometimes tell you to practice speaking in simple language. Human spirits in hell cannot understand complex ideas, and neither can animal spirits. They are absolutely clueless.

For instance, it is a backbreaking task to help a snake realize that it is dead. I personally experienced this years ago when I was once visited by the spirit of a dead snake. It was indeed very tough explaining to a snake spirit that it was dead. Even if you are able to convince a snake that it died after being run over by a truck, for example, it is still very challenging to teach a snake why it is wrong to possess humans as a way to escape their suffering. Would you be able to convince a snake with your current level of enlightenment?

The snake spirit possesses people because it has thoughts like, "I did nothing wrong. I was just slithering happily on a rainy road when a truck hit me out of the blue and killed me. It's not fair." How would you persuade such a resentful snake? How would you teach a snake that it is wrong to possess people? It is probably full of thoughts like "I didn't want to be killed." Would you be able to help the snake understand why it is wrong to think like that?

Considering the snake also had its own life, an effective way to guide it would be to start by talking through its life. For example, I would say, "You were such-and-such a snake and were born into such-and-such a place. You had a wife and children, but you died in this way in this place." Then, the snake would realize and think, "Oh, he is talking about me." If I talk about its feelings and say, "I suppose you are worried about your partner who is left behind," the snake may say, "That's right," and start opening up to me.

Even a snake opens up to you when it feels that it is being understood, and at this point, you can start guiding it. But if you insist one-sidedly that the snake is in the wrong, it will never accept its mistakes, no matter how hard you try to convince it.

The starting point of Kanjizai lies in the attitude of putting yourself in other people's shoes

At Happy Science, we often talk about how to save people or make people happy, but to do so, you must be able to put yourself in other people's shoes—this is the key point. Can you make observations based on other people's perspectives? Can you empathize with them? Only when you have such perspectives can you save others or make others happy in the truest sense.

Those who cannot put themselves in other people's shoes cannot truly make other people happy. I am not saying this as an abstract idea. For example, most lecturers and speakers are too focused on themselves when they give a speech or present research from a podium. They think about whether they can finish on time, which makes them tense and nervous. However, that is when they should think about the audience. They should observe how people are reacting to their speech and acknowledge what they are feeling.

Do you understand what I am trying to say? As a matter of fact, this is the heart of Kanjizai, or the starting point of Kanjizai. Even if you possess spiritual powers, if you do not have the tendency to see things from others' points of view, you will never be able to understand what people think and feel. While you may pick up things that benefit you, you will not be able to put yourself in other people's shoes.

Kanjizai is a "treasured sword" given to humans as proof that they are children of God

Many people claim to have spiritual powers simply because they can guess what is inside someone's wallet or predict the next day's weather, but to be frank, they do not know how to use their powers correctly.

Kanjizai is categorized as a spiritual power, but in a broader sense. Perhaps we can say that it is a developed form of spiritual power. Regardless of how we describe it, if we think about the reason why humans have the power of Kanjizai, we will eventually come to realize that it was given by God.

Kanjizai is granted to humans as a "treasured sword" or proof that they have truly awakened as a child of God. In reality, everyone possesses this "sword," but most people live out their lives without ever realizing it. Even if they do, they live their lives without knowing how to use it. In fact, only a few people are allowed to use this "sword."

Your power of Kanjizai becomes more apparent as you broaden your love

In this book, I explained that the power of Kanjizai begins to show its true potential when you reach the Brahma Realm. Although you might be able to use a rudimentary form of this power when you reach the highest level of the sixth dimension, it starts to reveal its true potential when you reach the Brahma Realm. Now, I would like you to think about the relationship between the initial stage of manifestation of Kanjizai and its corresponding stage of enlightenment.

What attribute begins to bud from the highest level of the sixth dimension? It is the next challenge or the goal for those who have reached the state of arhat. It is practiced at the level above arhat, and its true potential is exerted in the Brahma Realm. That is, of course, love.

The way love manifests is directly proportional to the manifestation of Kanjizai. Why is this so? In fact, the process of spiritual evolution from arhat to bodhisattva and then from bodhisattva to tathagata is related to how much you care about others. Caring about a large number of people suggests that your love is expanding. To put it another way, the more your love expands, the more people you will care about.

When your love develops and expands, and you want to practice it, what is required of you? When your love grows much larger than the love you have for your wife, your children, or the people close to you, what will you need to do? What is necessary when you wish to use your love on a grander scale to save people and create a great utopia? The answer is that you need to be able to understand the thoughts and feelings of many people. Wouldn't you agree? How can you love many people when you can only understand the feelings of people close to you and not those of others? Ultimately, the fact that your power of Kanjizai grows in alignment with your stage of enlightenment means that Kanjizai develops as your love does. This is what is at the root of Kanjizai.

3
The Difference in Values between the Front and the Rear Side of Heaven

Motive or result—which is more emphasized?

Now, let us think about the spirits who reside in the rear side of the heavenly world. These spirits practice love, indeed, but they do so in their own way. Their method is different from people like us who strive to think and act based on the Laws. They seek efficiency—which I mentioned at the beginning of this chapter—and they are mainly concerned with how to awaken people in an instant. For this reason, those in the rear side of heaven have a strong tendency to seek psychic power itself.

Those who belong to the rear side are spiritual, indeed. When they are living in the earthly world, many of them work in fortune-telling and divination, and their motives are often rooted in good intentions. In other words, they want to instantly awaken people to the spiritual world, or awaken them spiritually, by telling them how they have lived their life without any prior information. This is also a form of love expressed in their own unique way.

Then, what is the difference between the love of the spirits in rear heaven and front heaven? There is clearly a huge difference between the two. When the spirits in rear heaven manage to awaken people by using their psychic powers, they tend to be overtaken by pride. They have a habit of confirming the result and savoring it. They tend to relish the fact that they achieved wonderful results through their own powers. Spirits in rear heaven possess such an attribute.

What about spirits who belong to the worlds of bodhisattva and tathagata, or who reside in front heaven? Their main focus is on their motive. This is the biggest difference. They value the motive over receiving credit for results, and they strive to save and love people simply because they want to do so. They do not seek happiness from having the results of their actions attributed to them. They do not help others out of a desire to benefit themselves or to take credit for the results. They practice love for the sake of love. They have transcended self-interest and do not seek to take anything for themselves from the results of their actions. They are overflowing with love. They are filled with overwhelming love.

From this, we can see that what distinguishes the front and the rear side of heaven is the difference in motives behind the thoughts and actions of the spirits that reside there, which are the two important factors in practicing Buddha's Truth. I must say that thoughts are more valued in the Real World; thoughts or motives are considered to be more important.

While spirits in front heaven place less emphasis on the actions or the results of actions, spirits in rear heaven value them more.

When these spirits are born into the earthly world, how will they differ? In fact, even high spirits express different tendencies when they are born into this world, depending on whether they come from the front side or the rear side of heaven. For example, those from the front side conduct acts of love and altruism because they like to do so or because doing so makes them happy. They strongly feel that taking actions for the sake of others is their calling and that it is part of their personality. They naturally behave this way because it is what they wish to do. On the other hand, those from the rear side are more concerned about how the results of their actions will reflect on them. They mainly focus on how good the outcome is or what positive effect their actions will bring. In this way, there are two types of spiritual tendencies.

Exploring the Will of God in terms of thoughts, actions, and results

Now, the question is, what is God's view on the difference between the front and the rear sides of heaven? God follows the process of "from thoughts to actions to results." So ultimately, He places great value on thoughts.

Then, what is the outcome or result? What does the result mean to the highest-dimensional being? Let us say again that this being exists in the twentieth dimension. As described in Chapter Three, suppose this twentieth-dimensional existence expresses itself as nineteenth-dimensional existences, which are then reflected by nineteenth-dimensional mirrors to manifest as eighteenth-dimensional beings, and so on. What this shows is that in the Spirit World, the results or outcome produced by actions are on the "outskirts," that is, the farthest from God.

Let us assume that the twentieth-dimensional being is the origin of everything, or thought that exists in the twentieth dimension. When this thought brings action, it appears in the nineteenth dimension, and when this being in the nineteen dimension brings action, it appears in the eighteenth dimension. This continues into the seventeenth dimension, and so on, until the third dimension appears, which is the world unfolding right before our eyes. Based on this idea, we can see that out of the three processes of thought, action, and result, thought is closest to God. Thought is the closest to God, followed by action, and then result.

People who first seek results, which lie farthest from God, are considered to be on the outskirts of the world created by

God. But God did not originally create humans as beings of that nature. Hence, people who judge things based on the outskirts, in other words, results, have an earthly way of thinking. Such people who focus on results have a strong inclination towards earthly views. On the other hand, those with less inclination towards earthly values focus on actions and behaviors, and those who are even more detached from earthly thinking focus on thoughts. This is the difference between them.

Therefore, result-oriented people or those who are overly concerned about results have a strong tendency to approach things from the farthest end of the world created by God, in other words, from a viewpoint farthest away from Him. On the other hand, people who are more focused on their thoughts can see themselves, others, and the world from a perspective that is closest to God's. Put simply, we can say that people who place more importance on thoughts are more spiritually awakened.

How are thoughts, actions, and results related to the multi-dimensional structure?

In the multi-dimensional structure of the Spirit World, thoughts, actions, and results are manifested differently. For example, even within the Tathagata Realm of the eighth dimension, there is the front side and the rear side, which includes the realms of *sennin* (hermit) and *tengu* (long-nosed goblin). You may wonder why there are such distinctions between the worlds of the spirits, even though they are at the same spiritual level.

✦ The conical structure of the Earth's multi-dimensional world

The truth is, the world we live in, or the Earth Spirit Group, has a conical structure, where the light shines from a single point. In higher dimensions, there is greater emphasis on thoughts, while in lower dimensions, there is less emphasis on thoughts and more emphasis on actions and results. If you look at each dimension separately, such as the ninth dimension and then the eighth dimension, you will find that the upper realms of the Spirit World put more weight on thoughts and little weight on actions and results. On the other hand, the more you move down the dimensions, the more weight is placed on actions and results rather than thoughts. In the earthly world, even less emphasis is placed on thoughts.

In short, you will know what kind of person you are by looking at what you focus on when recognizing yourself or the world around you. Very few people identify themselves as a manifestation of their own thoughts while they are alive. Only a few people believe that they are what they think about. Most people believe that the figure reflected in the mirror is who they are. Or perhaps they recognize themselves by comparing themselves to others, such as their husband, children, parents, and friends, and by interacting with them. They see the world around them as an environment that consists of length, width, and height. People with this worldview may only be able to see this world as such, but seen from the Real World, the third dimension is actually a world of plentiful sediment, as it places very little emphasis on thoughts but large emphasis on actions or results that arise from thoughts; from the spiritual point of view, actions and results settle heavily at the bottom. Humans are living in such a kind of world.

✦ The metaphor of a flask and starch

When you look down at the worlds below from the twentieth dimension, you will see that the thoughts emitted from the highest dimension descend to the lower dimensions. It is like starch sinking to the bottom of water in a large flask.

Suppose you heat the bottom of the flask that is filled with water. The water at the bottom gradually gets hot while the water near the top remains cool. Now, if you drop some starch from the mouth of the flask, it gradually sinks to the bottom because it is denser than water. The starch at the top remains partially liquid while the starch near the bottom turns translucent and solidifies little by little, like thin porridge. This metaphor is similar to how I perceive the world. Ordinary people cannot see the world in this way, but I can see how the world looks from far beyond. To me, the world looks like starch powder falling into a flask from above and solidifying near the bottom.

Spirits in the Tengu and Sennin Realms focus on results

So, how should we imagine "the world close to God"? In terms of the metaphor I used, the liquid part that has not yet solidified represents the original world that is closest to God, whereas the part that gradually settles, solidifies, and hardens symbolizes the lower dimensions.

God's thoughts are pure at the origin, but begin to take on human attributes from the ninth dimension. Solidification then begins in the Tathagata Realm of the eighth dimension. As you go down the world of human spirits, God's thoughts gradually solidify more, which means spirits focus more on actions and results. This tendency begins to show in spirits of the eighth dimension, and this world is known as the "rear side."

To put it another way, the Sennin and Tengu Realms in the eighth dimension are a projection of the third-dimensional world that is located in the eighth dimension. The spiritual grade of spirits who reside there may be at the eighth-dimensional level, but they have an extremely strong tendency to think in an earthly way. What this means is that there are spirits who heavily focus on the results of the sequence of thoughts, actions, and results. Spirits with earthly tendencies not only reside in the eighth dimension but also in the seventh dimension and below. The lower in dimension you go, the more of them there are, which means there are many more of such spirits in the sixth dimension than in the seventh. When seen from a spiritual perspective, what originally started as a pure thought solidifies in the lower dimensions; it turns into something "non-fluid" and "solid."

Therefore, we can say that the area known as the rear side of the Spirit World starts in the dimensions where human attributes are mixed into one's spiritual worldview.

4
The Tenth-Dimensional World and the Great River of Time

The tenth-dimensional consciousnesses are the beginning of individuality

Now, let's move on to the tenth dimension and think about what kind of world it is. In the tenth dimension of the Earth, there are currently three spirits—the Grand Sun Consciousness, the Moon Consciousness, and the Earth Consciousness—and each of them has its own characteristics and ways of thinking. The differences in their characteristics and thinking bring about a pattern of action and achievements unique to each spirit. So from the tenth dimension, spirits start to show individuality. In other words, the different purposes and roles of these three consciousnesses in the tenth dimension mark the beginning of individuality. When one's purpose and role become more specific, the spirits will acquire more human-like characters, like the ninth-dimensional spirits.

The Grand Sun Consciousness governs positivity

In my teachings, I have been explaining that the Grand Sun Consciousness governs positivity, or *yang*. By hearing so, you probably just believe it. But I would like you to take a moment and imagine the vast galaxy or the great universe floating infinitely far away. Imagine a thirteenth-dimensional Cosmic Spirit or an even higher-dimensional being looking at the panorama of the great universe expanding in front of it. (Author's note: The El Cantare consciousness is at or above the level of thirteenth-dimensional Cosmic Spirit when He interacts with the messiahs of the universe.) If you were this high-dimensional spirit, why do you think the consciousness of positivity or yang exists in the great universe?

The power of positivity is not necessarily associated directly with the existence of the universe itself. It exists because of a Will that commands, "Let there be positivity." It is the power that actively pushes everything forward, the power that provides the world with a life force, and the power that gives the world heat and energy. This power does not simply exist coincidentally or naturally; it is an extremely mysterious force. Would you have ever come to know that such an amazing force is at work in this universe without studying or being taught about it?

The Sun continuously gives off limitless heat and energy, regardless of whether humans are aware of it or not, because it knows that it is wonderful to do so. It knows that giving off heat and energy is meaningful work. If the Sun were not aware of the importance of this work, there would be no heat or energy.

The Moon Consciousness governs elegance, negativity, harmony, and femininity

The Earth also has the Moon Consciousness, which I have been explaining as the one that governs the aspects of elegance, negativity, harmony, and femininity. When you observe the panoramic view of the great universe, you may wonder where the artistic and harmonious elements come from. The truth is that they have also manifested through the Will of El Cantare Consciousness, which values these qualities.

The Earth Consciousness provides a field and space

Last but not least, there is the Earth Consciousness. (Author's note: The Earth Consciousness is close to El Cantare, when He is referred to as the God of the Earth.) This is a consciousness that provides a suitable environment. So, in a sense, it is the consciousness of a "field." It is a consciousness that provides all beings with a field or a space to exist. The history of the Earth began when this consciousness provided space and time began to flow within it.

Two disparate positions are required for time to flow

The two elements that make up time are the Grand Sun Consciousness and the Moon Consciousness. Time started flowing thanks to the active and passive elements of *yang* and *yin*, or vigor and elegance.

Then, do you know why something is able to flow? It is because of the disparity that exists between the two elements. A disparity between the two elements, such as high and low, right and left, or up and down, gives birth to a flow. Just as water falls from a dam, a river flows from upstream to downstream, or a waterway runs from right to left, a flow begins when there are two elements in different positions.

How time looks from the perspective of God

It is the *yang* consciousness and *yin* consciousness that created the two polarities in the space of this great universe. These two consciousnesses are the reason for two polarities to exist and for a current called time to have started flowing between them. Time contains all the creation, development, and growth in the great universe.

You may think that various civilizations and events rise and fall or flourish and wane, and that time flows through them, but that is not how I see it. In my eyes, there is a flow of time, which contains various events. I see time differently from how people normally do. From my perspective, time flows like a great river or like the Milky Way. I can see the great river of time flowing in this vast galaxy. If I look at it closely, I can see the rise and fall of various civilizations and those of various planets flowing in the "water" of the great river of time. So, it is time that contains the rise and fall of civilizations, not the other way around. What I see is the river of time that contains various events.

This is how God sees the history of humankind and the universe. The way He sees things differs from how humans see them. In the eyes of God, the universe is a panoramic view with a river called time running through it. To start the river of time, God created two polarities: *yang* and *yin*. Because of these two polarities, a disparity appeared, which allowed time to flow in the space between them. Everything is contained within the flow of time.

What does the great universe look like?

Then, what is it that we call the "past, present, and future"? Can you guess what it is? In the eyes of God, what we call the "past, present, and future" is just like what flows between the poles of a magnet placed on a table. The table represents the expanse of the great universe. The universe, which seems to have a multi-dimensional structure in the eyes of humans, is nothing more than a table from the perspective of God. In this table-like space, God created two polarities. One was the *yang* consciousness or the consciousness of positivity. It lets things flow out, creates things, and gives birth to things, and that is why there was a need for something that can receive whatever it produces. Thus, God created the *yin* consciousness as a receiver. These two consciousnesses are like the north and south poles of a magnet or the positive and negative electrodes of a battery. He created a pole from which things flow and a pole that receives them. That was when a magnetic force began to flow between them.

You have probably seen a diagram with magnetic field lines running from the north pole to the south pole, on both the upper side and lower side of a magnet. If I were to explain how God looks at the history of the great universe, it would be as though the history and the flow of time all take place within the bounds of these magnetic field lines. Everything starts from the north pole and reaches the south pole, and then disappears. This is how God sees the history of the great universe.

Now, imagine magnetic field lines being drawn in the air using iron sand. It would look as though the iron sand is moving along these lines. It is as simple as that. The iron sand keeps moving in a cycle based on the law of cause and effect, also known as the law of causality. In this world of magnetic field lines, humans come up with various ideas like good, evil,

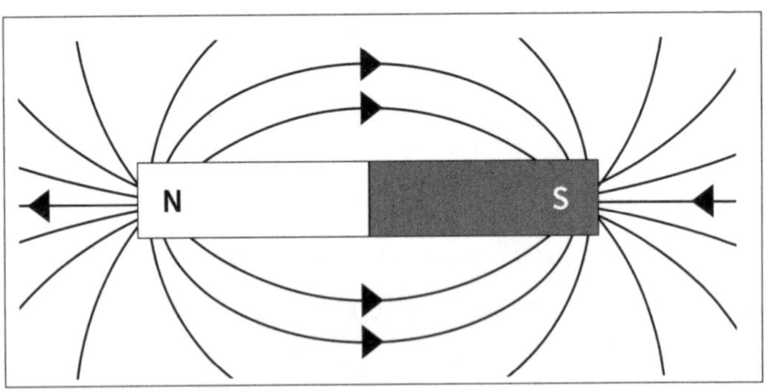

A diagram depicting magnetic field lines around a bar magnet. They appear when you scatter iron sand around the bar magnet, and they extend from the north pole in all directions and curve back to the south pole.

truth, and beauty, and confirm for themselves the meaning of each grain of iron sand. Each grain represents, for example, a way of thinking that is part of the framework of the Laws, and when expressed as a three-dimensional entity, it represents things like our galaxy, the Solar System, or the Earth.

5
The Source of Kanjizai

The stars and planets in the great universe and the Spirit Worlds surrounding them

Now, what exactly do I mean by "iron sand" and the "magnetic field around the iron sand"? Let me use a more concrete example to make it easier to understand. Suppose grains of iron sand are floating in the air within these magnetic fields, and one of the grains represents the Earth. This grain is not just an ordinary grain of iron sand, but a grain with a magnetic field around it. It is surrounded by a special energy field, although it is small. This field of energy, or the special energy field around the grain of iron sand, that is, the Earth, is what we call the "Spirit World." This is the structure of our world.

Each world is a magnetic field surrounding a grain of iron sand. There are various magnetic fields, and each of them is extremely similar to the "parent" magnetic field that is created by positivity and passivity, or yang and yin. But even so, they have slightly different characteristics from each other. Thus, the various stars and planets that exist in the great universe and their Spirit Worlds are actually small grains of iron sand with special magnetic fields surrounding them. This is the phenomenon that takes place in each universe.

This is a simplified explanation to enable you to understand, but seen from a much grander perspective, the very universe that humans recognize is also a grain of iron sand. The grain refers to what we call the thirteenth-dimensional universe, which has its own magnetic field. Other universes also have their own magnetic fields. This is how the fourteenth-dimensional consciousness sees the various universes. There are also other universes that are different from our thirteenth-dimensional universe. Regardless, they all share a similar type of magnetic field created between "electrodes."

The world as seen by a fourteenth-dimensional consciousness

So far, I have been giving you various explanations to tell you about God, His Will, and the world He created, but they are not mentioned in the prior chapters of this book. All of you people are looking at the world from your own perspective, someone of less than seven feet tall. Because you look at things from a fixed perspective of the earthly, third-dimensional world, you only understand things from the third-dimensional perspective. You look at the result first, and then actions, and then thoughts. However, if you look at the world from God's perspective, it looks as I just described. You will see a magnet with two poles on a table, iron sand moving and flowing in the air between the poles, and a magnetic field forming around those grains of iron sand. You will also see the characteristics of each magnetic field. This roughly describes the enlightenment of a fourteenth-dimensional being.

The reason I can explain this much is that I draw spiritual current from that world. A consciousness of the fourteenth dimension is like an electrical current, and it flows into me. When I look at the current, I can see its source and where it comes from. Simply put, I can see the world that a fourteenth-dimensional consciousness sees. I can do this because I have an "antenna" that catches the "radio wave" conveying this vision.

Being in tune with the consciousness that created the great universe

What exactly does it mean to be able to send or receive this kind of radio wave? This is actually what Kanjizai is all about. Considering Kanjizai within the framework of human consciousness, its fundamental power or ultimate power represents in the ability to be in tune with the consciousness that created the great universe. By tuning yourself into it, you can see what it sees.

When you have the ability to see outer space or the Earth moving as iron sand in a magnetic field, all psychic powers that are perceived through the senses of human eye feel insignificant. Even Nyoshin, the ability that enables you to perceive things through "multiple eyes," feels like a completely basic and rudimentary power. At the ultimate level of Kanjizai, your eyes themselves expand tremendously to see the universe. So, whether you have multiple eyes or just one eye becomes a trivial matter. With the power of Kanjizai, your awareness itself can expand infinitely. This is the unique characteristic of Kanjizai; it is an ability that enables you to connect to the ultimate consciousness of the universe.

The relationship between Kanjizai and Rojin

What, then, is the power of Rojin? When you draw "electricity" into the third dimension through the power lines connected to the ultimate part of the universe, you need an "insulator" to prevent an electrical leakage. That is where Rojin comes in. When you live with an awareness of Kanjizai, you will find it difficult to lead a normal life. That is why you need "insulation" to avoid "electrocuting" yourself. This insulation is called the power of Rojin.

I explained Rojin and Kanjizai as having vectors pointing inward and outward, respectively. But the truth is that Kanjizai is a huge pillar that exists in the vast space of this great universe, and Rojin is a branch that extends from this huge pillar, or trunk, down to the ground. So, Kanjizai, the trunk, is much, much bigger than the power of Rojin.

This is roughly what I have to say about Kanjizai.

AFTERWORD

How did you feel after reading this book? I am sure you felt that a truly mysterious world is unfolding before you as you turned the pages. When you unravel the secrets of the universe like I did in this book, you cannot help but wonder about the true purpose of spiritual powers.

Having said so, real spiritual powers are nothing like those possessed by mere street-level psychics or minor religious leaders. Rather, they are a fighting tool bestowed upon us from God to illuminate future society, and to reveal what lies beyond the modern physics that started with Einstein.

In no way am I overstating when I say that the ideas contained in this book clearly disclose the world that lies beyond Einstein's theories of special and general relativity. In this respect, I humbly believe that I have succeeded in transcending or surpassing the wall that separates the worlds of religion and science. I would be more delighted than ever if this book successfully proves that true religion is science itself.

Ryuho Okawa
Master & CEO of Happy Science Group
September 1988

For a deeper understanding of
Kanjizai, Buddha's Omniscient Power of Perception
see other books below by Ryuho Okawa:

The Laws of the Sun [New York: IRH Press, 2018]

Rojin, Buddha's Mystical Power [New York: IRH Press, 2021]

The Eternal Buddha [New York: IRH Press, 2024]

What Is Happy Science? [New York: IRH Press, 2023]

ABOUT THE AUTHOR

Founder and CEO of Happy Science Group.

Ryuho Okawa was born on July 7th, 1956, in Tokushima, Japan. After graduating from the University of Tokyo with a law degree, he joined a Tokyo-based trading company. While working at its New York headquarters, he studied international finance at the Graduate Center of the City University of New York. In 1981, he attained Great Enlightenment and became aware that he is El Cantare with a mission to bring salvation to all humankind.

In 1986, he established Happy Science. It now has members in 185 countries across the world, with more than 700 branches and temples, as well as 10,000 missionary houses around the world.

He has given over 3,500 lectures (of which more than 150 are in English) and published over 3,250 books (of which more than 600 are Spiritual Interview Series), and many are translated into 42 languages. Along with *The Laws of the Sun* and *The Laws of Hell*, many of the books have become best sellers or million sellers. To date, Happy Science has produced 28 movies under his supervision. He has given the original story and concept and is also the Executive Producer. He has also composed music and written lyrics for over 450 pieces.

Moreover, he is the Founder of Happy Science University and Happy Science Academy (Junior and Senior High School), Founder and President of the Happiness Realization Party, Founder and Honorary Headmaster of Happy Science Institute of Government and Management, Founder of IRH Press Co., Ltd., and the Chairperson of NEW STAR PRODUCTION Co., Ltd. and ARI Production Co., Ltd.

BOOKS BY RYUHO OKAWA

Related Books

THE LAWS OF THE SUN

ONE SOURCE, ONE PLANET, ONE PEOPLE

ISBN: 978-1-942125-43-3 • $15.95

Why and how did God create this world? What is a spirit and soul? For what purpose are humans living in this world? How can we find true happiness and meaning in life?

The Laws of the Sun answers life's questions humans have always had throughout history.

In this book, Ryuho Okawa outlines the laws that govern the universe and provides a road map for living one's life with greater purpose and meaning.

The Truth taught in this book will significantly transform your life and allow you to develop love and acceptance toward people of all races and religions.

ROJIN, BUDDHA'S MYSTICAL POWER

ITS ULTIMATE ATTAINMENT IN TODAY'S WORLD

ISBN: 978-1-942125-82-2 • $16.95

In this book, Ryuho Okawa has redefined the traditional Buddhist term *Rojin* and explained that in modern society, it means the following: the ability for individuals with great spiritual powers to live in the world as people with common sense while using their abilities to the optimal level. This book will unravel the mystery of the mind and lead you to the path to enlightenment.

The Laws of Eternity

El Cantare Unveils the Structure of the Spirit World

ISBN: 978-1-958655-16-0 • $17.95

Where do we come from, and where do we go after death?

The Laws of Eternity answers life's most important questions that we are all confronted with at some point or another.

Author Ryuho Okawa takes us on a journey to the other world, a place where we came from before we were born and return to after death.

Open its pages and discover the eternal mysteries and the ultimate secrets of Earth's spirit group that have been covered by the veil of legends and myths.

THE LAWS OF FAITH

ONE WORLD BEYOND DIFFERENCES

ISBN: 978-1-942125-34-1 • $15.95

Since antiquity, religion has played a pivotal role in human development. However, today's society favors logical reasoning, leaving many to stray away from spiritual progress. This is likely due to traditional religions failing to provide concise answers to modern-day problems.

A religious leader, Master Ryuho Okawa, preaches the core teachings of the world religion and the faith in the God of Earth. By integrating logical and spiritual viewpoints, Okawa gives answers to modern-day problems that traditional religions cannot solve.

Inside this book, you will find teachings that will truly unite the world as one.

THE TRUTH ABOUT EARTH, THE UNIVERSE, THE SPIRIT WORLD

LIFE'S Q&A WITH EL CANTARE

ISBN: 978-1-958655-26-9 • $17.95

This is a compilation of 28 Q&A sessions conducted by author Ryuho Okawa, where he answers numerous intricate questions varying from the theory of evolution to the creation of the multidimensional universe, all without a script.

While the non-existence of the spirit or the Spirit World has never been definitively proven, Okawa provides profound yet clear answers.

By delving into this eye-opening book, you will gain a renewed perspective on your life and the world around you.

UFO Reading Light vs. Darkness

The Clashing Values of the Universe

ISBN: 978-4-8233-0454-5 • $15.95

There are actually many UFOs flying above us. You may have seen one before, or what you thought was a star may indeed have been a UFO. Through his spiritual abilities, spiritual master and world teacher Ryuho Okawa revealed that an unseen battle over the values of good and evil has been taking place between different species of space people.

The Novel The Shaking

ISBN: 978-4-8233-0451-4 • $16.95

This novel revolves around a psychic, Principal Shohei Reiwa of Happy Christ School (HCS). The story starts with a mysterious incident that occurs at the school in the middle of the night. Using his spiritual abilities, Reiwa learns the shocking truth behind the incident. To solve it, he summons five HCS students who are fit for this mission. Little did they know, the incident would lead to an unimaginable opponent and the discovery of the secret of the universe.

Bestselling Buddhist Titles

THE ESSENCE OF BUDDHA

THE PATH TO ENLIGHTENMENT

ISBN: 978-1-942125-06-8 • $14.95

The essence of Shakyamuni Buddha's original teachings of the mind are explained in simple words. Through this book, you will learn how to attain inner happiness, the wisdom to conquer ego, and to enter the path to enlightenment.

THE CHALLENGE OF THE MIND

AN ESSENTIAL GUIDE TO BUDDHA'S TEACHINGS: ZEN, KARMA AND ENLIGHTENMENT

ISBN: 978-1-942125-45-7 • $16.95

In this book, Ryuho Okawa explains essential Buddhist tenets and how to put them into practice. He offers a solid basis of reason and an intellectual understanding of Buddhist concepts.

THE LAWS OF GREAT ENLIGHTENMENT

ALWAYS WALK WITH BUDDHA

ISBN: 978-1-942125-62-4 • $17.95

Discover the power of forgiveness from Buddha's enlightenment and compassion, and the true relationship of work and enlightenment. In addition, the author reveals his own experience when he attained the Great Enlightenment.

THE ETERNAL BUDDHA

NOW, HERE, IS THE IMPERISHABLE LIGHT

ISBN: 978-1-958655-19-1 • $17.95

Embedded in this book is a message from Eternal Buddha, the parent of your soul. You will discover the true origin of your soul, why you have chosen to be born in this time, and why having faith is important.

THE TRUE EIGHTFOLD PATH

GUIDEPOSTS FOR SELF-INNOVATION

ISBN: 978-1-942125-80-8 • $16.95

This book explains how we can apply the Eightfold Path, one of the main pillars of Shakyamuni Buddha's teachings, as everyday guideposts in the modern age to achieve self-innovation to live better and make positive changes in these uncertain times.

THE CHALLENGE OF ENLIGHTENMENT

NOW, HERE, THE NEW DHARMA WHEEL TURNS

ISBN: 978-1-942125-92-1 • $17.95

What is the role of enlightenment in facing the challenges of the modern world? By reading this book, your mind becomes clearer and learns to savor inner peace, and you will be empowered to make profound life improvements.

ONE MORE STEP FORWARD

THE INVINCIBLE THINKING TO GET YOU THROUGH TOUGH TIMES

ISBN: 978-1-958655-25-2 • $17.95

Success in life is determined not by our circumstances but by our mindset and how we think.

In this book, author Ryuho Okawa reveals from his first-hand experience how the spirit of self-help can create new values.

Okawa is a true self-made man with an indomitable spirit to bring happiness to all humankind. His drive to keep moving forward by taking steady steps through the power of discipline has led to the publication of over 3,200 books in 37 years (at the time of its publication).

Unlock the keys to lifelong growth and success by reading this book.

True Bushido Spoken By Ame-no-Mioya-Gami

The Japanese Father God Teaches How We Should Live and Die

ISBN: 978-4823304606 • $20.00

Nearly 30,000 years ago, Ame-no-Mioya-Gami (The Japanese Father God) descended on the foothills of Mt. Fuji in a fleet of spaceships. He taught the values of Justice, Prosperity, Order, and Harmony, which are the original Japanese spirit. In this book, Ame-no-Mioya-Gami speaks on the true meaning behind bushido and why people must regain the samurai spirit.

Be Infinitely Kind

For We Are Living in the Great River of Love

ISBN: 978-1-958655276 • $17.95

What is true love? What is the true definition of kindness? In this book, Ryuho Okawa invites readers to explore the deeper spiritual virtues of love and kindness—essential qualities for building strong, lasting relationships with those we hold dear. Truthfully, the more love we give, the wealthier our souls become.

THE TEN PRINCIPLES FROM EL CANTARE VOLUME I

RYUHO OKAWA'S FIRST LECTURES ON HIS BASIC TEACHINGS

ISBN: 978-1-942125-85-3 • $16.95

How did Happy Science begin? What are its teachings? What is its aim? This is a compilation of early lectures that built the foundation of Happy Science. The historic moments are captured in this book.

THE TEN PRINCIPLES FROM EL CANTARE VOLUME II

RYUHO OKAWA'S FIRST LECTURES ON HIS WISH TO SAVE THE WORLD

ISBN: 978-1-942125-86-0 • $16.95

Volume II contains passionate messages of Ryuho Okawa filled with the wish to save humankind and build utopia on earth. You can also learn about God's three major inventions, the mission of religion, and more.

What Is Happy Science?

Best Selection of Ryuho Okawa's Early Lectures (Volume 1)

ISBN: 978-1-942125-99-0 • $17.95

The Best Selection series is a collection of Ryuho Okawa's passionate lectures from the ages of 32 to 33 that reveal the mission and goal of Happy Science. *Volume 1* teaches the eternal Truth, including the meaning of life, the secret of the mind, the true meaning of love, the mystery of the universe, and how to end hatred and world conflicts.

The Way to Human Perfection

Best Selection of Ryuho Okawa's Early Lectures (Volume 2)

ISBN: 978-1-958655-20-7 • $17.95

The path to enlightenment starts from understanding 'the eternal viewpoint of life.' By recognizing that we have eternal life, we can realize that caring and bringing joy to others are the keys to true happiness and success.

WHO IS EL CANTARE?

El Cantare means "the Light of the Earth." He is the Supreme God of the Earth who has been guiding humankind since the beginning of Genesis, and He is the Creator of the universe. He is whom Jesus called Father and Muhammad called Allah, and He is *Ame-no-Mioya-Gami*, the Japanese Father God. He is also known as Vishnu in India and Tiandi in China. Different parts of El Cantare's core consciousness have descended to Earth in the past, once as Alpha and another as Elohim. His branch spirits, such as Shakyamuni Buddha and Hermes, have descended to Earth many times and helped to flourish many civilizations. To build a new civilization on Earth by uniting various religions and integrating various fields of study, a part of the core consciousness has now descended as Master Ryuho Okawa.

Alpha is a part of the core consciousness of El Cantare, who descended to Earth around 330 million years ago. Alpha preached Earth's Truths to harmonize and unify Earth-born humans and space people who came from other planets.

Elohim is a part of the core consciousness of El Cantare, who descended to Earth around 150 million years ago. He gave wisdom, mainly on the differences between light and darkness, good and evil.

Ame-no-Mioya-Gami (The Japanese Father God) is a Being who is close to the core consciousness of Lord El Cantare, and is the Creator God and the Father God who appears in ancient literature, *Hotsuma Tsutae*. It is believed that He descended on the foothills of Mt. Fuji about 30,000 years ago and built the Fuji dynasty, which is the root of the Japanese civilization. With justice as the central pillar, Ame-no-Mioya-Gami's teachings spread to ancient civilizations of other countries in the world.

Shakyamuni Buddha was born in Nepal around 2,600 years ago as the prince of the Shakya clan. When he was 29 years old, he renounced the world and sought enlightenment. He later attained Great Enlightenment and spent most of his life in India teaching and practicing the Truth. He is the founder of Buddhism, which has spread extensively throughout Asia.

Hermes is one of the 12 Olympian gods in Greek mythology, but the spiritual Truth is that he taught the teachings of love and progress around 4,300 years ago, which became the origin of the current Western civilization. He is a hero who truly existed.

Ophealis was born in Greece around 6,500 years ago and was the leader who went on an expedition as far as Egypt. He is the God of miracles, prosperity, and arts, and is known as Osiris in Egyptian mythology.

Rient Arl Croud was born as a king of the ancient Incan Empire around 7,000 years ago and taught about the mysteries of the mind. In the heavenly world, he is responsible for the interactions that take place between Earth and various planets.

Thoth was an almighty leader who built the golden age of the Atlantic civilization around 12,000 years ago. In Egyptian mythology, he is known as God Thoth.

Ra Mu was a leader who built the golden age of the civilization of Mu around 17,000 years ago. As a religious leader and a politician, he ruled by uniting religion and politics.

ABOUT HAPPY SCIENCE

Happy Science is a religious group founded on the faith in El Cantare, who is the God of the Earth and the Creator of the universe. The true essence of human beings is an eternal soul created by God, and we go through the cycle of reincarnation to train and develop our souls. We have been carrying out various activities to spread this spiritual value and build a peaceful and prosperous world that God wishes. At Happy Science, we explore righteousness, in other words, God's Will. This is called the "Exploration of Right Mind." More specifically, it means to practice the Fourfold Path: Love, Wisdom, Self-Reflection, and Progress. This is the path that leads humans to attain happiness that carries over from this world to the next.

Love–practicing "love that gives"
To give love to others without expecting anything in return is the starting point of happiness. By practicing "love that gives," you will become closer to God.

Wisdom—studying spiritual truth
By studying the Truth, you will be able to distinguish good and evil, live righteously, and learn the heart of God. True wisdom leads people to true happiness.

Self-Reflection—correcting your mistakes
Self-reflection is the act of correcting wrongful thoughts and actions you have accumulated during the day and regaining the pure, true nature of the soul.

Progress—creating utopia on earth
True progress is about spreading happiness to others and improving society as you achieve your own success. This will create utopia on earth.

PLACES OF WORSHIP FOR HAPPY SCIENCE

Shoja

—A PLACE TO REFINE YOUR MIND, GAIN SPIRITUAL WISDOM, AND BE REBORN

Happy Science shoja (temple) is a sacred spiritual field where you can deepen your faith and heighten your enlightenment. Under the spiritual guidance of high spirits, shoja holds various seminars to improve individual character and practices ritual prayers to help believers solve their life problems and make progress. By participating in them, you can regain the peaceful and blissful mind that you may have lost in your everyday life.

27 SHOJAS IN JAPAN AND 3 SHOJAS WORLDWIDE

Sohonzan Shoshinkan

Sohonzan Miraikan

Holy Land El Cantare Seitankan

Tokyo Shoshinkan

Australia Shoshinkan

Brazil Shoshinkan

San Francisco

Local Branch

—A PLACE TO CHANGE YOUR DESTINY

Since 1986, Happy Science has been carrying out various activities to produce people who can truly say, "I am happy." At our local branches, many new believers are being born and are leading better lives through faith in Lord God El Cantare. All kinds of events take place here, such as lecture viewing, book seminars, prayers, and counseling sessions. Everyone is welcome!

HAPPY SCIENCE'S ENGLISH SUTRA

"The True Words Spoken By Buddha"

"The True Words Spoken By Buddha" is an English sutra given directly from the spirit of Shakyamuni Buddha, who is a part of Master Ryuho Okawa's subconscious. The words in this sutra are not of a mere human being but are the words of God or Buddha sent directly from the ninth dimension, which is the highest realm of the Earth's Spirit World.

"The True Words Spoken By Buddha" is an essential sutra for us to connect and live with God or Buddha's Will as our own.

MEMBERSHIPS

MEMBERSHIP

If you would like to know more about Happy Science, please consider becoming a member. Those who pledge to believe in Lord El Cantare and wish to learn more can join us.

When you become a member, you will receive the following sutras: "The True Words Spoken By Buddha," "Prayer to the Lord," and "Prayer to Guardian and Guiding Spirits."

DEVOTEE MEMBER

If you would like to learn the teachings of Happy Science and walk the path of faith, become a Devotee member who pledges devotion to the Three Treasures, which are Buddha, Dharma, and Sangha. Buddha refers to Lord El Cantare, Master Ryuho Okawa. Dharma refers to Master Ryuho Okawa's teachings. Sangha refers to Happy Science. Devoting to the Three Treasures will let your Buddha nature shine, and you will enter the path to attain true freedom of the mind.

Becoming a devotee means you become Buddha's disciple. You will discipline your mind and act to bring happiness to society.

EMAIL OR **PHONE CALL**

Please turn to the contact information page.

ONLINE member.happy-science.org/signup/

CONTACT INFORMATION

Happy Science is a worldwide organization with branches and temples around the globe. For full details, visit happy-science.org. The following are some of our main Happy Science locations:

United States and Canada

New York
79 Franklin St., New York, NY 10013, USA
Phone: 1-212-343-7972
Fax: 1-212-343-7973
Email: ny@happy-science.org
Website: happyscience-usa.org

New Jersey
66 Hudson St., #2R, Hoboken, NJ 07030, USA
Phone: 1-201-313-0127
Email: nj@happy-science.org
Website: happyscience-usa.org

Chicago
33 West Higgins Rd. 4040,
South Barrington, IL 60010, USA
Phone: 1-630-937-3077
Email: chicago@happy-science.org
Website: happyscience-usa.org

Florida
5208 8th St., Zephyrhills, FL 33542, USA
Phone: 1-813-715-0000
Fax: 1-813-715-0010
Email: florida@happy-science.org
Website: happyscience-usa.org

Atlanta
1874 Piedmont Ave., NE Suite 360-C
Atlanta, GA 30324, USA
Phone: 1-404-892-7770
Email: atlanta@happy-science.org
Website: happyscience-usa.org

San Francisco
525 Clinton St.
Redwood City, CA 94062, USA
Phone & Fax: 1-650-363-2777
Email: sf@happy-science.org
Website: happyscience-usa.org

Los Angeles
1590 E. Del Mar Blvd., Pasadena,
CA 91106, USA
Phone: 1-626-395-7775
Fax: 1-626-395-7776
Email: la@happy-science.org
Website: happyscience-usa.org

Orange County
16541 Gothard St. Suite 104
Huntington Beach, CA 92647
Phone: 1-714-659-1501
Email: oc@happy-science.org
Website: happyscience-usa.org

San Diego
7841 Balboa Ave. Suite #202
San Diego, CA 92111, USA
Phone: 1-626-395-7775
Fax: 1-626-395-7776
E-mail: sandiego@happy-science.org
Website: happyscience-usa.org

Hawaii
Phone: 1-808-591-9772
Fax: 1-808-591-9776
Email: hi@happy-science.org
Website: happyscience-usa.org

Kauai
3343 Kanakolu Street, Suite 5
Lihue, HI 96766, USA
Phone: 1-808-822-7007
Fax: 1-808-822-6007
Email: kauai-hi@happy-science.org
Website: happyscience-usa.org

Toronto
845 The Queensway
Etobicoke, ON, M8Z 1N6, Canada
Phone: 1-416-901-3747
Email: toronto@happy-science.org
Website: happy-science.ca

Vancouver
#201-2607 East 49th Avenue,
Vancouver, BC, V5S 1J9, Canada
Phone: 1-604-437-7735
Fax: 1-604-437-7764
Email: vancouver@happy-science.org
Website: happy-science.ca

WORLDWIDE

Tokyo
1-6-7 Togoshi, Shinagawa,
Tokyo, 142-0041, Japan
Phone: 81-3-6384-5770
Fax: 81-3-6384-5776
Email: tokyo@happy-science.org
Website: happy-science.org

London
3 Margaret St.
London, W1W 8RE United Kingdom
Phone: 44-20-7323-9255
Fax: 44-20-7323-9344
Email: eu@happy-science.org
Website: www.happyscience-uk.org

Sydney
516 Pacific Highway, Lane Cove North,
2066 NSW, Australia
Phone: 61-2-9411-2877
Fax: 61-2-9411-2822
Email: sydney@happy-science.org

Sao Paulo
Rua. Domingos de Morais 1154,
Vila Mariana, Sao Paulo SP
CEP 04010-100, Brazil
Phone: 55-11-5088-3800
Email: sp@happy-science.org
Website: happyscience.com.br

Jundiai
Rua Congo, 447, Jd. Bonfiglioli
Jundiai-CEP, 13207-340, Brazil
Phone: 55-11-4587-5952
Email: jundiai@happy-science.org

Seoul
74, Sadang-ro 27-gil,
Dongjak-gu, Seoul, Korea
Phone: 82-2-3478-8777
Fax: 82-2-3478-9777
Email: korea@happy-science.org

Taipei
No. 89, Lane 155, Dunhua N. Road,
Songshan District, Taipei City 105, Taiwan
Phone: 886-2-2719-9377
Fax: 886-2-2719-5570
Email: taiwan@happy-science.org

Taichung
No. 146, Minzu Rd., Central Dist.,
Taichung City 400001, Taiwan
Phone: 886-4-22233777
Email: taichung@happy-science.org

Kuala Lumpur
No 22A, Block 2, Jalil Link Jalan Jalil Jaya
2, Bukit Jalil 57000,
Kuala Lumpur, Malaysia
Phone: 60-3-8998-7877
Fax: 60-3-8998-7977
Email: malaysia@happy-science.org
Website: happyscience.org.my

Kathmandu
Kathmandu Metropolitan City,
Ward No. 15, Ring Road, Kimdol,
Sitapaila Kathmandu, Nepal
Phone: 977-1-537-2931
Email: nepal@happy-science.org

Kampala
Plot 877 Rubaga Road, Kampala
P.O. Box 34130 Kampala, Uganda
Email: uganda@happy-science.org

ABOUT IRH PRESS USA INC.

Founded in 2013, New York-based IRH Press USA Inc. is the North American affiliate of IRH Press Co., Ltd., Japan. The Press exclusively publishes comprehensive titles on Spiritual Truth, religious enrichment, Buddhism, personal growth, and contemporary commentary by Ryuho Okawa, the author of more than 3,250 unique publications, with hundreds of millions of copies sold worldwide. For more information, visit Okawabooks.com.

Follow us on:

- Facebook: Okawa Books
- Instagram: OkawaBooks
- Youtube: Okawa Books
- Twitter: Okawa Books
- Pinterest: Okawa Books
- Goodreads: Ryuho Okawa

NEWSLETTER

To receive book-related news, promotions, and events, please subscribe to our newsletter below.

irhpress.com/pages/subscribe

AUDIO / VISUAL MEDIA

YOUTUBE

PODCAST

Visit the above to learn more about Ryuho Okawa's books. Topics range from self-help, current affairs, spirituality, religion, and the universe.